"This book revolutionized the way we relate to visitors and is fueling a new wave of growth in our congregation. This is the most practical book I've read on making the church into the kind of community that embraces new people."   **United Methodist Minister**

"Thanks for this wonderful book. Our adult and youth Sunday school classes all studied it, and it's transforming our church."
                    Church of the Brethren Minister

"Bernhard and Clapp provide practical ideas that can increase the quality of hospitality. . . . This book has great value for pastors and the entire church."
                    Herb Miller in *Net Results*

"Christian Community provides a wealth of resources that should be made available to local churches. This book is current, to the point, and easy to read."
                    Ivan George, American Baptist Churches

"This is a very practical book that will help local churches who are serious about their caring and about their outreach."
                    Loren Mead, Founder of The Alban Institute

"Our church has never been comfortable talking about evangelism, but the hospitality approach fits us very well. Studying this book has helped us learn how to do outreach in a way that fits our congregational culture."
                    United Church of Christ Minister

About Fred and Steve's book
Hospitality: Life in a Time of Fear:

"The best benefit from studying this book has been the difference made in the personal lives of study participants. This book teaches you how to look at the world through the eyes of Christ."   **Lutheran Minister**

"This book gave a new perspective to me and to many in our church. Hospitality can transform how you drive, how you relate to clerks in stores, how you live with your family, . . . "   **Episcopal Church Minister**

"This valuable new release deals directly with the tough questions raised by the tragic events of September 11, 2001. . . . recognizing the presence of Christ in others can have a liberating impact on all we do."
Church Educator

"The book can be used by pastors who must deal with the undercurrent of fear in our society. . . . and church leaders who simply want to make their church more hospitable to strangers."   *Net Results*

"This book will help you find meaning and purpose in a fearful world and equip people to extend healing and hope to others living in fear."
Sheila Hoover in *Leadership Development*

"How can the church function in an environment of fragmentation, violence, and fear? This book takes a practical approach, offering many excellent suggestions to congregations grappling to show hospitality in our complex time."   *Mennonite Weekly*

Contents

Rather than a traditional table of contents, we've chosen to include not only the chapter titles but also the core concept covered in each chapter.

3

This book is dedicated to:

Jesus Christ, from whose invitation I experience God's welcome, acceptance, and the affirmation of my person-hood; and who confirmed for me that, by God's grace, I have been adopted into God's family.

My family:
— spouse, Joice
— daughter, Barbara, and sons, Howard and Tom; their spouses, Wayne, Patty, and Melodie
— grandchildren, Kimberly and spouse Cary; Lori; Carrie; Robert; Melissa (deceased); Rachel; and Michael
— our great-grandchildren, David and Jordan

They daily teach me how to live in an hospitable relational environment as a microcosm of God's family.

The Oakland Congregation, a covenanted body of people, whose dedication and practice allowed this book to become a reality. In our journey together, we came to believe that the welcome and acceptance we experienced in Christ must be shared with the outsider until all people experience that same welcome and acceptance— and hear Christ's invitation to become sons and daughters in God's glorious family.

Fred Bernhard

And to:

The Church Universal, that great company of saints who belong to the body of Christ and whose reality transcends denomination, race, nation, culture, time, and space. That Church which shows hospitality to all people, in all times, and in all places.

My brothers and sisters in Christ at Lincolnshire Church who have embraced me from the moment of my arrival in Fort Wayne and who continue to renew my faith.

Steve Clapp

We both extend our thanks for the contributions made to this book by: Paul Mundey, Barb Faga, Karen Carlson, Carolyn Egolf, Holly Sprunger, Kristen Leverton Helbert, Claire Long, Christine Brewer, Barbara Menke, Jerry Peterson, Stacey Sellers, and the staff of Evangel Press.

Welcome one another, therefore, just as Christ has welcomed you, for the glory of God.

Romans 15:7

Our Expectations Were Too Low—
Introduction to the Fourth Edition

Over fifty years ago, C.S. Lewis wrote that "God not only wishes to bless us, God wishes to bless us beyond what our minds can imagine or conceive." While it is a serious mistake to overestimate what we ourselves are capable of doing, which leads us to the sin of pride, it is easy to underestimate what God can make possible. God continually seeks to bless our lives and the lives of those around us.

The two of us were introduced to each other by our mutual friend Paul Mundey, who was at that time the director of The Andrew Center. Paul thought we should collaborate on a book about hospitality and hoped that we would like each other. It has now been almost a decade since that introduction, and we both cherish the wonderful friendship that has developed between us in the process of working together. We not only collaborated on this book, *Widening the Welcome of Your Church*, but went on to write two other books together: *Hospitality: Life in a Time of Fear* and *Worship and Hospitality*.

Response to *Widening the Welcome of Your Church* has far exceeded our expectations. The book has been reprinted multiple times, and we made some modest revisions in the second and third editions. People have continued to purchase the book and have been gracious enough to invite us to conduct workshops and consultations in many congregations and regional judicatories (conferences, districts, synods, dioceses, presbyteries, areas). We've seen church-wide study of this book bring about significant renewal in congregations across the country.

We concluded that the time had come for a more substantial revision than was done with the second or third editions. Our hope is that this new edition will be an improved resource both for those who have not read this title before and for those who have previously studied an earlier edition.

The religious landscape is changing, and there is no shortage of interpreters and commentators on those changes. Speakers and authors around the country have talked about what it means to live in a postmodern society and have made pertinent observations about how to reach out to those without a church connection. Natural Church Development has become a popular means of looking at the health of congregations across the country and around the world.

Technology continues to transform our society and the way that we do our work and even develop our friendships. Many congregations are finding creative uses for the innovations of our time including:

- The development of websites for use by members and as a possible outreach tool to the unchurched.

- The use of e-mail for the sharing of prayer requests, devotions, and the minutes of meetings.

- The use of satellite television connections to conduct classes and workshops.

- The widespread use of cell phones which lets clergy and other church staff be almost instantly available for pastoral emergencies.

We celebrate the ways in which all of these perspectives and strategies have improved our ministries. We have been surprised in some ways that interest in hospitality has continued to be so strong. The concept of biblical hospitality does not have the instant pizzazz of postmodern discussions or Natural Church Development or the Internet. But the lack of pizzazz is part of the reason that interest remains so strong.

Biblical hospitality is not just another philosophical explanation or strategy for growth and improvement. Biblical hospitality is core to the church and something we should practice every day of our lives. Biblical hospitality is not something that we should practice because it will make our churches grow. It is something we should practice because it is how our Lord wants us to live with one another both in the church and in the larger community. Church growth is a byproduct of hospitality, not the reason for it.

Hospitality is not just a matter of how warmly we welcome those who visit our congregations, of how much we smile and how well we remember the names of guests. Those things are important, but they are only the surface manifestations of true biblical hospitality. Hospitality truly has the power to transform our view of ourselves, our guests, our congregations, and our communities. For people living in this post 9/11 world, it is an especially strong source of power and renewal for our lives and our churches.

This newly revised edition continues the same careful look at the biblical basis for hospitality and the practical implications of it that were in the three previous versions. In this edition, we also:

- Include some new examples of how hospitality has been meaningfully demonstrated in congregations.

- Consider more fully what it means to live in a world that feels less safe because of the events of September 11, 2001.

- Deal more forthrightly with the implications of biblical hospitality for how we relate to persons with a non-heterosexual orientation and to persons who are not married but are in sexual relationships with each other.

- Reflect deepened appreciation for how vital it is for congregations to be educated about hospitality and outreach. The practice of hospitality and the sharing of the faith come naturally to a few of us but require significant education for most.

- Make suggestions for congregational surveys and other strategies to better assess just how hospitable our congregations really are. Based on the congregational studies we conducted over the last decade, we are sadly convinced that most of our churches are not nearly as welcoming as members and pastors think they are.

Two of the themes in this book receive a fuller treatment in our other books. *Hospitality: Life in a Time of Fear* was written in

11

responsé to the trauma of September 11, 2001. In that book, we show that the answer to fear is not turning inward but turning outward. Learning to recognize the presence of Christ in others can have a liberating impact on all that we do. *Hospitality: Life in a Time of Fear* looks at the biblical and spiritual roots of hospitality, offers suggestions for deepening the spiritual life, and shows how a life of prayer is essential to a life of hospitality. The book explores the implications of hospitality not only for our congregations but also for our family life, for friendships, for our places of work, for our roles as drivers of automobiles, and for our relationship to the suffering of the world.

Worship and Hospitality takes a careful look at the implications of hospitality for the practice of worship. We live in a time of rapid change in worship, with words like informal, alternative, contemporary, and experimental being used to describe services that are not traditional. Many congregations struggle to determine whether to offer a variety of styles of worship through different services or to use services that blend both traditional and contemporary elements. The lens of hospitality has the power to transform our view of worship because it motivates us to look at the experience of worship not simply from the viewpoint of our own preferences and desires but through the viewpoint of the needs and struggles of others.

Many people who are reading these words have had times of significant discouragement with the institutional church. Some are discouraged because of continued decline in membership and attendance. Some are discouraged because there are large categories of persons who are not welcomed in their congregations. Some are discouraged because the quality of congregational life is not deeper and better. We offer this book in the sincere belief that God is at work seeking to bless all of our lives and all of our congregations.

We have had the privilege of seeing many congregations and many individuals transformed through a deepened understanding and practice of biblical hospitality. May the same be true for you and your church. May your expectations be raised and exceeded.

Fred and Steve

Hospitality:
Not Optional and Not Safe

Concept: In a society filled with both rational and irrational fear, God calls us to embrace the stranger, to recognize the presence of Christ in the one who is unknown. Hospitality is not an option for the church, and it is not always safe.

"World Trade Center and Pentagon Destroyed—Thousands Perish"

"Search Continues for Missing Child"

"New Wave of Break-ins in Pine Valley"

"Vandalism at All-Time High"

"Gun Ownership Continues to Climb"

We've all read and heard the headlines—in newspapers and magazines, on radio and television, and through Internet services. We don't feel safe as a society, and not all that fear is irrational!

Most of us were riveted to our television sets on September 11, 2001 and the days that followed. The tragedy of that day has dramatically raised our awareness of our vulnerability as individuals and as a society.

This book, however, grows out of a conviction that the way of Christ is different from the way of the world. We do not want to live foolishly, but we do want to live consistently with what our Lord has taught us. In a society increasingly filled with fear and distrust, people are hungry for the kind of acceptance and intimacy that the church, at its best, offers.

Many of us form our basic attitudes toward the unknown in general and toward strangers in particular during our childhood years. Fred and Steve were both blessed with early experiences that helped them feel confident about their well-being and comfortable with strangers.

We want our respective contributions to this book, for the most part, to appear seamless, for there to be no abrupt shifts from person to person in narration, and for the identification of whether it is Fred or Steve speaking to be irrelevant. As we begin our account, however, we each want to share childhood stories.

Roots in Childhood

Fred: My family lived on a farm in Pennsylvania along the main thoroughfare between Harrisburg and Lancaster. Hoboes, as we called them, made frequent visits to our farm for hot meals and overnight lodging. I came to understand the aid my parents gave travelers as a Christian practice and learned to enjoy contact with these strangers. Curiosity led me to explore who they were, why they were transients, and why they chose our farm to request meals and lodging. The memory of those shabbily dressed persons wearily trudging up our farm lane, with knapsacks slung over their stooped shoulders and canes in hand, evokes a pleasant and precious nostalgia.

On Sundays my parents would invite other church families to our home for dinner. I grew up seeing this practice as an integral part of the Sunday worship experience. The people with whom we shared in worship were also our friends.

Likewise, visitors to church were invited home for a sumptuous noon meal and encouraged to spend the afternoon in conversation. Lodging would be offered if the visitor had come from a distance.

Newcomers to our community would also be invited into our home for a meal. While they were with us, we would inquire about their religious affiliation, and depending on their answer, would extend a general or specific invitation to worship with our family if that was appropriate. We would witness to the faith we held but only at the point of their inquiry; it never occurred to us to attempt to force our belief on others.

14

If these newcomers had not yet accepted Christ as Lord and Savior, that invitation would certainly be extended to them at the appropriate point—but not apart from the context of regular worship and Bible study. This gradual incorporation allowed newcomers to know who we were and what was expected of them before a commitment was made.

For my family, practicing hospitality was an end in itself. It was an expression to others of our thanks to God for Christ's generosity to us. This faith-sharing often led others to a commitment to discipleship, but that was viewed by us as a by-product of our need to respond to them in a loving manner. The hobo, the visitor, and the newcomer received our gifts as the outward expression of our faith.

Part of the reason that my parents were so effective in extending hospitality is that they knew what it meant to be a stranger. Their Brethren beliefs were considered somewhat peculiar and were unpopular in the larger community. The rejection they had experienced enabled them to better understand the sense of isolation that others could experience.

Steve: My childhood experiences were different from Fred's in terms of geography and denomination. I grew up in downstate Illinois and spent my childhood and teenage years in the Methodist (now United Methodist) Church. My experiences with strangers, however, were remarkably similar to those of Fred.

My father was the township supervisor for the community in which we lived. That meant, among other things, that he was responsible for all the aid and relief which was given to persons who were unemployed or homeless or just passing through town. People for whom the forces of life had been difficult came to our home, seeking help from my father. What they encountered has little in common with how such assistance is given through government agencies today. My father's greeting to them was always warm and personal, and he made it clear that he was glad they had come. He would invite them to join us for a meal, and he taught me to relate to them as to any other guests in our home. There were no forms for them to fill out, and there was no waiting period for receiving assistance.

15

I can remember some of my friends at school being shocked when they occasionally discovered that we had people who were known alcoholics, ex-convicts, and transients visiting us. Some of their parents talked about the fact that my father and mother didn't seem to use good judgment in differentiating between those who were simply "down on their luck" and those who were "the root of their own problem." I can certainly remember my father urging some to start attending A.A. meetings, and I cannot even count the number of times he made calls to arrange temporary housing and to open the door for employment. But I do not remember his ever barring anyone from our dinner table or sending out into the night anyone who did not have a place to stay. I remember his treating everyone with considerable graciousness and kindness, and I remember the transforming effect that had on many lives.

My parents likewise extended a warm welcome to persons who visited our church and to persons who were new in the community. In part because the town was small enough for "everyone to know everyone" (or at least to think that they did!), local residents were pulled between enormous curiosity about and an almost irrational distrust of those who were newly arrived. My parents, however, had both moved there from other places and knew what it was like to come as a stranger.

Both my parents had been raised in the church, and the Bible was extremely important in their lives. One of my father's favorite passages of Scripture was Matthew 25:31–46 about encountering Christ "in the least of these."

Living in Fear

Flying has become a very different experience since 9/11. The relatively small airport from which Steve departs for most of his business travel does not, as of the date of this writing, have the kind of technology that performs a quick and automated screening of luggage. Each time he checks luggage for a flight, he has to stand and watch while a security officer opens and searches through his suitcase. This act has to be relatively boring for the security officer (since Steve rarely has anything interesting in his bag), but it feels extremely invasive to have another person looking through one's possessions.

16

Most of those reading this book know the airport security drill. The screening process continues with walking through a metal detector and the screening of carry-on items. Like hundreds of thousands of others, Steve and Fred have learned to automatically remove their shoes to avoid any possibility of setting off the metal detector and getting pulled aside for further screening. Both Steve and Fred feel particular empathy for those persons who receive an extra level of screening because of the misfortune of an artificial limb or joint that sets off the metal detector. It also seems to Steve at his home airport that a disproportionate number of persons in their seventies and eighties get pulled aside for extra screening, though they appear to be the most unlikely terrorists imaginable.

At the end of the screening process, when things aren't too busy, the last security officer will sometimes say: "Thank you. Have a nice day." Those words lend a certain civility to the process, but it seems very inconsistent to have a person who has just treated you as a potential terrorist invite you to have a nice day.

At one level, some of us are relieved by the existence of the heightened security procedures and feel safer as a result. At another level, many of us suspect that the procedures are only adequate to dehumanize us and make us more suspicious of one another but not at all sufficient to protect us from a well planned terrorist attack. Indeed it is doubtful that any security procedures are fully adequate to protect us.

In many respects, fear and distrust seem to have spread like a cancer in our land. Symbols of openness are disappearing from the North American scene as we barricade ourselves from strangers in an effort to protect ourselves and our possessions. Electronic door locks on cars, double and triple locks on house doors, security alarms, guard dogs, lobby guards, security officers, increased numbers of police, and the military are just a few signs of our deep-seated fear of the stranger. We hide our money, lock our doors, chain our bikes, and look over our shoulders.

We know the fear of having car trouble on the highway and not having anyone stop. We know the anxiety of trying to find our way around an unfamiliar neighborhood or city.

News reports of break-ins, break-outs, and blackouts feed our fears. We have come to view strangers more as potential enemies than as potential friends. We keep our eyes on our luggage and pocketbooks as we travel. We may feel sympathy for the hitchhiker or the stranded motorist, but most of the time we keep driving. When we park in a shopping mall lot, we lock our valuables in the trunk, away from the eyes of strangers. We are often victimized by our fears, instinctively avoiding persons who look or speak differently than we do.

All of our social institutions have been affected by the growth of fear in our society. Churches, once known as havens of refuge and houses of prayer, now lock the doors to the very persons to whom they claim to minister. In response to highly publicized, truly horrible instances of student violence, our schools now post guards to protect students from students and teachers from students. Drug-sniffing dogs and metal detectors have become standard operating procedure in many schools. Many office buildings and large companies have significantly increased sec-urity, some requiring registration of everyone who enters.

Certainly statistics on violent crime justify a cautious approach to certain situations. Yet it is one thing to live with a reasonable sense of caution and another entirely to have most of one's existence determined by fear. Instead of risking new possibilities for ourselves and the stranger, too many of us continue hiding behind our walls, lamenting the world's condition. By failing to come to know the stranger, we too often make that person an enemy rather than a friend.

Visiting Churches

Most of us like to think of our congregations as warm and welcoming. Yet the reality is that our discomfort with strangers often carries over into the life of the church.

On three different occasions, Fred experienced significantly less than a warm welcome in visiting congregations on Sunday mornings. In one church, while seated in a pew with his wife, Fred heard someone whispering about them from four pews away: "Who's that? What are they doing here?" Fred, unin-timidated, went back to the two people who had been whispering and introduced himself. As he walked back to his own seat, he heard one of them say to the other: "And just who is Fred Bernhard?" In another congregation, he was actually asked to move out of a seat that a member felt was permanently reserved! In the third congregation, he had the experience of not being spoken to by anyone. Fred Bernhard does not, in Steve's opinion, appear threatening or intimidating—in fact, it would be very difficult not to like Fred.

During a tenure in church bureaucracy and years of consulting, Steve has visited a large number of congregations across North America. He has uniformly experienced enthusiastic welcomes from congregations when serving as a guest speaker or sharing a consultant's report. When his role and identity are not clearly known, however, the response has sometimes been very different. He has frequently stood drinking coffee by himself during the "fellowship time" between worship and Sunday school, while congregation members gathered in cliques. In one large congregation, he was even asked to mop a restroom floor by a pastor who did not know he was a visitor instead of a member.

There are a few congregations with name tags that give the number of years the person has belonged to the church. While the use of name tags is generally a significant help to hospitality in a congregation, the identification of years of membership on the tags sends a very negative message to visitors and new members. The practice suggests: "Those of us who have been here a long time are more important than those who are new."

Being asked to get out of "someone else's seat," being ignored by everyone else present, and being asked to mop a floor are not the kinds of welcomes that make people want to return to a congregation. To have such things happen is an abomination to the Christ we serve. We do not own the pews, and we do not own the church. Christ gave his life for us and also for the stranger we encounter in the church or in the community.

The drawing by Kimberly J. Haugh at the beginning of this book was inspired by Romans 15:7. People who journey to the cross welcome, accept, and affirm one another. The cross symbolizes both our ultimate acceptance through Jesus Christ's crucifixion and also our call to unconditionally accept one another.

19

In his letter to the Romans, Paul makes it clear that the Gospel is not just for the Jewish people, those who have been circumcised, the insiders. The Gospel is for everyone. In Romans 15:12, he quotes Isaiah: "'The root of Jesse shall come, the one who rises to rule the Gentiles; in him the Gentiles shall hope.'"

The Future of the Church

Many people are in the midst of a love-hate relationship with the Christian church. As Richard Kew and Roger J. White describe feelings toward their own Episcopal Church: "We see its warts and blemishes all too clearly, yet even while it infuriates us, we cherish it" [*New Millennium, New Church*, p. 89]. Some of us are bothered because the church is too slow to change; others are distressed because the church seems to embrace new trends and causes without regard for the role which tradition has played. Some are offended because of the church's involvement in what they consider political matters, but others are disappointed by the apparent irrelevancy of the church to the problems of society.

Ken Gibble writes in *The Messenger*: "It is no accident that we don't always agree on things—whether it be politics or theology or the church budget. For reasons God alone knows, God gives us people to live with who sometimes make us want to pull our hair out in frustration. . . .

"As someone has suggested, in the church we do not choose who our fellow members will be. And that's a good thing, because if we could choose, our choices would be limited by self-serving motives. Instead, in the church, in any true community, our companions are given to us by God's grace. Often they will be the very people who will upset our cherished view of ourselves and the world" [p. 21]. Loving the church means loving those who are part of it, and that is not always an easy task. Sometimes it isn't easy to love ourselves!

When our feelings about the church and brothers and sisters in the church are mixed, we can understandably feel overwhelmed about the possibility of welcoming the stranger. But difficulty in welcoming the stranger can also come from those of us who are pleased and excited by our involvement in the local church. Sometimes our needs are met at such a high level by the existing people and programs of a congregation that we have difficulty accepting change in what serves us so well. Having new members, however, means change for the church. Thus even those without mixed feelings toward the church may find themselves reluctant to embrace the stranger, without fully understanding why.

No matter how we feel toward the church, there is, we believe, no escaping the reality that we are called to welcome the stranger and to seek out those who are not part of the Christian community. If we wait to solve all of our internal ecclesiastical problems before we embrace the outsider, some of us will be waiting until the second coming. If we let ourselves remain so self-satisfied or focused on our own needs that we do not truly welcome new people, we will restrict the church's potential and shut ourselves off from the gifts God seeks to provide through new relationships. The persons who are at first strangers in the church may mean:

- more people for the bell choir
- new teachers for Sunday school
- less burnout for present members
- friends to stand with us when life is hard
- new perspective on our problems as individuals and the church.

The future of many congregations appears dim if persons cannot learn how to better appreciate one another and to celebrate rather than lament their differences. Growth for our churches is simply not viable unless we learn how to embrace those who are strangers. As long as we let our Christian walk be governed by the fears that grip the rest of society, we will find ourselves unsettled by strangers and unable to make friendship the normal expectation when we encounter new people.

Hospitality

The word hospitality is not new. We practice it in various ways as part of everyday life. At times, especially with those we already know and trust or know through others, we model it almost perfectly. We speak of southern hospitality and under-stand the meaning of "hospitality rooms" and "hospitality

21

suites." We use the word to describe persons who exhibit extraordinary graciousness. Being hospitable is for some the opposite of being rude. The word also evokes images of tea parties, pleasant conversations, and an aura of coziness.

The meaning and explanation of hospitality, however, go deeper than those images. The experience and practice of hospitality lies at the very core of what it means to be a Christian. Its roots are woven into the foundation of Judaism and Christianity. An old Hebrew proverb notes that "hospitality to strangers is greater than reverence for the name of God" [Robert E. Meagher in "Stranger at the Gate" in *Parabola 2*].

In the New Testament, the Letter to the Hebrews makes clear the importance of hospitality: "Do not neglect to show hospitality to strangers, for by doing that some have entertained angels without knowing it" [13:2]. In the first three editions of this book, we offered the following definitions of hospitality and of the stranger:

> **Hospitality** is the **attitude** and **practice** of providing the **atmosphere** and **opportunities**, however risky, in which strangers are free to become friends, thereby feeling accepted, included, and loved. The relationship thus opens up the possibility for eventual communion among the host, the stranger, and God.
>
> The **stranger** is any person or group not known to the host. The host perceives that this unknown person or group has the potential for relationship as an enemy or as a friend.

In our book *Hospitality: Life in a Time of Fear*, we offered an additional definition:

> **Hospitality** involves recognizing the presence of Christ in family, friends, coworkers, neighbors, and complete strangers. It means responding to others as we would respond to the presence of Christ in our midst.

Hospitality is not something optional for the church. It is in fact the very essence of the church's life and witness. As you learn to improve your practice of hospitality, you will find relationships transformed not only with the stranger but also with those in the body of Christ you already know and with your friends and family. **Widening the Welcome of Your Church** means learning how to practice the biblical art of hospitality, to recognize the presence of Christ in the stranger, and to build transforming relationships.

Hospitality is not itself a strategy for church growth, but if you truly learn how to practice it, your church will grow. A congregation that practices biblical hospitality will be filled with passion and vitality and will develop a caring, inviting personality. Your own life will be enriched as well with new friendships, the joy of more energy in the congregation, and a closer relationship with Christ. People will be pulled toward you and toward your congregation. When members of a church start becoming excited about hospitality, others want to be part of it.

As you read and study the pages that follow, you'll gain an increasingly deep sense of what hospitality means and of its implications for your congregation. **Hospitality is not optional,** and the better you understand it, the more you will want to keep practicing it in the ways outlined in this book.

Remember, however, that hospitality is not always safe. There's a small chance that someone we choose to befriend will turn out to be manipulative or dishonest. We may occasionally extend hospitality toward those who will reject us. We may find that the practice of hospitality leads us into contact with persons we would otherwise have avoided.

And possibly the most distinct and frightening danger of all is that practicing hospitality may change our lives.

"Lord, when was it that we saw you hungry or thirsty or a stranger or naked or sick or in prison, and did not take care of you?"

Then he will answer them, "Truly I tell you, just as you did not do it to one of the least of these, you did not do it to me."

Matthew 25:45–46

A Biblical Look at Hospitality

> **Concept:** The Old and New Testaments both regard hospitality as an obligation. The biblical texts do not question the worthiness of the needy stranger but instead examine the faithfulness of the one from whom hospitality is needed.

In contemporary North America, those of us with sufficient financial resources find travel an exciting and not overly difficult process. A person living in Indiana or Ohio, where the two authors of this book make their homes, can board an airplane in a snowstorm on a winter morning and be in the warmth of California or Florida before noon. Comfortable automobiles, buses, and trains provide other transportation options.

Restaurants proliferate at an astounding rate, and so many of them are chains that one knows what to expect in a new city before walking through the door. Hotels and motels provide reasonably comfortable accommodations, and telephones, fax machines, dataports, and even wireless connections in guest rooms make it easy to stay in touch with home. Those who want more variety and who treasure the unique can abandon the big chains and select bed and breakfasts and one-of-a-kind restaurants.

Maps are readily available, and there are information centers at the entrances to most states and recreational areas. Bookstores contain all kinds of directories of attractions, lodging, and restaurants around North America and around the world. Technology has made life even easier with so much information available from Internet searches, travel reservations easily made through the Internet, and directions available from MapQuest and other online services. Sophisticated navigational systems in some automobiles make it very easy to find one's way across the country.

The traveler in the Ancient Near East faced radically different circumstances. No one traveled unless absolutely necessary. There was no Bedouin Disneyland, and the concept of travel for pleasure or education would have seemed absurd. With the exception of a few cities, public places of accommodation were not available. In this environment, the practice of hospitality truly made the difference between life and death for the sojourner.

Hospitality in the Orient

People throughout the Mediterranean world regarded the provision of food, lodging, and protection as a virtue and sacred duty. The following were common components of the act of hospitality:

- **Bowing:** In receiving a desert guest, the host would often bend at the knees and gradually lower his or her body until touching the ground. This act revealed the host's desire to render the highest possible honor to the stranger-guest.

- **Feet-washing:** People wore sandals, and a day on the desert meant dirty, hot, and often sore feet. Washing the feet was an act of kindness which conveyed honor to the guest.

- **Preparing and serving food:** The host might devote considerable time and expense to preparing food for the guest. The generous Bedouins were known to deny themselves for the sake of the guest. The host's family ate later from what remained. The thoughtful guest always left a portion of food on the dish.

- **Needs of animals:** The host also provided the needed food and lodging for the camels of the guest.

- **All guests were seen as potential friends:** Obviously the stranger can represent a friend or an enemy, but the starting assumption in the Ancient Near East was that the stranger was a potential friend. Names were not exchanged until after the meal was eaten, if at all. An exchange of names and background information was not considered a requirement for hospitality.

The stranger could also expect protection from the host. If a stranger was being pursued by an enemy, the fleeing person only had to touch the peg of the host's tent to be safe. The pursuer would be forced to peer helplessly from outside the tent while the guest was entertained. That protection generally extended for thirty-six hours, the period thought to be sustained by a meal or the time needed for salt to leave the stomach. That length of time permitted a headstart for the fugitive. Psalm 23 takes on new meaning when one thinks about the tradition of hospitality in relationship to these words:

> *You prepare a table before me*
> *in the presence of my enemies;*
> *you anoint my head with oil;*
> *my cup overflows.*

Abraham and Hospitality

Genesis 18:1–15 describes the hospitality of Abraham toward three men who appeared near the entrance to his tent. Biblical scholars (including Vawter, Von Rad, and Fretheim) agree that the three strangers are personages of Yahweh, though we are not clear in precisely what way. In *The New Interpreter's Bible*, Terence Fretheim offers this perspective: "From the narrator's point of view, Yahweh appears to Abraham at his home (v.1). From Abraham's point of view, however, three men stand near him (v.2). Yahweh has assumed human form appearing among the three men; the other two are angelic attendants" [Volume I, p. 462–463]. Consider the text:

> *The Lord appeared to Abraham by the oaks of Mamre,*
> *as he sat at the entrance of his tent in the heat of the*
> *day. He looked up and saw three men standing near*
> *him. When he saw them, he ran from the tent entrance*
> *to meet them, and bowed down to the ground. He said,*
> *"My lord, if I find favor with you, do not pass by your*
> *servant. Let a little water be brought, and wash your*
> *feet, and rest yourselves under the tree. Let me bring a*
> *little bread, that you may refresh yourselves, and after*
> *that you may pass on—since you have come to your*
> *servant."*

> *So they said, "Do as you have said." And Abraham hastened into the tent to Sarah, and said, "Make ready quickly three measures of choice flour, knead it, and make cakes." Abraham ran to the herd, and took a calf, tender and good, and gave it to the servant, who hastened to prepare it. Then he took curds and milk and the calf that he had prepared, and set it before them; and he stood by them under the tree while they ate.* **Genesis 18:1–8**

Abraham offers hospitality without being aware of the divine presence. That hospitality is consistent with the practice in the Ancient Near East and includes these elements:

- Abraham bows to them.

- Abraham offers them water, rest, and food.

- They accept.

- The meal is prepared and includes a calf, which would have been reserved for a special occasion, and butter, which was greatly prized by the nomad.

- Abraham waits on them while they eat.

- The strangers did not reveal their identity nor did they offer any gift or payment prior to the meal.

In sharing the calf and the butter, Abraham and Sarah gave far more than custom required. They chose to treat the three men as honored guests, and they did so without expecting anything in return. In verses 9–15, one of them tells Sarah that she will have a son. The fact that the gift of a child was promised can be seen as a response to their hospitality, but the promise of a son had already been made in the preceding chapter. The hospitality existed for its own sake, and Abraham has been lifted up as a model because of it. Had Abraham and Sarah refused hospitality to the strangers, they would have shut themselves off from the blessings God intended—not just the blessing of a son but also the blessing of God's presence.

Other Old Testament Examples

A full overview of all the biblical references to hospitality goes beyond the space or scope of this book. There are many other passages worthy of exploration. The following list is not an exhaustive one:

- Numbers 35:9–15 describes **cities of refuge.** These were refugee centers for Levites who needed protection from revenge until receiving a trial. They also offered safe havens for strangers who needed protection from enemies.

- In Job 31:32, as part of his **defense of his innocence,** Job speaks of his practice of providing food and lodging for the stranger.

- **Breaches of hospitality** are described in:
  — Deuteronomy 23:3–4
  — Judges 4:11–21; 5:24–27; 8:5–7; 19:15, 24
  — 1 Samuel 25:2–38
  — Isaiah 32:5–8

- The **provision of food** is described in:
  — 1 Samuel 9:22
  — 2 Samuel 9:7
  — 1 Kings 4:22; 10:5a
  — Nehemiah 5:17a

- **Requirements of the law** include:
  — Exodus 22:21; 23:9
  — Leviticus 19:10
  — Deuteronomy 10:19; 23:24–25

Jesus and Hospitality

In the New Testament, we find the practice of hospitality directly linked to its practice in Judaism. As in the Old Testament passages, the New Testament accounts do not focus the issue on the worthiness of the stranger but rather on the faithfulness of the one from whom hospitality is sought. Several passages give helpful perspectives to us:

- **Matthew 26:6–13** gives an account of Jesus in the home of Simon the leper. Going to the home of a leper would have been unacceptable to the religious establishment, but Jesus does so without hesitation. While he is there, a woman pours a costly ointment on his head, showing a hospitality which foreshadows his burial.

- **Luke 10:29–37** tells the Parable of the Good Samaritan. This well-known parable answers the important question: "Who is my neighbor?" The parable strongly reinforces that all people are our neighbors, and the obligation to care for others cuts across all religious, ethnic, and economic lines.

- **Luke 14:12–24** includes the Parable of the Great Dinner, in which Jesus advocates that the one who extends hospitality invite "the poor, the crippled, the lame, and the blind. And you will be blessed, because they cannot repay you, for you will be repaid at the resurrection of the righteous" [v.13–14].

- **Luke 19:1–10** shows Jesus again with one of the people the religious authorities ,would have avoided—this time with Zacchaeus the tax collector. A similar reference is found in **Luke 5:27–32** in which Jesus eats with "a large crowd of tax collectors" [v.29].

- **John 13:1–20** describes Jesus' washing the feet of the disciples at the time of the Last Supper. Jesus not only accepted the hospitality of others, but he also displayed hospitality through his entire ministry. The ritual or ordinance of washing the feet of another goes back to the custom in the Ancient Near East and is a clear affirmation of the value put on the one who is the guest.

The Least of These

Matthew 25:31–46 presents an account very similar in some ways to that in Genesis 18, studied earlier. We are told to reach out to those who are hungry, naked, homeless, or imprisoned. When we show hospitality to such persons, it is as though the kindness was actually being shown to Christ:

> *"Lord, when was it that we saw you hungry or thirsty or a stranger or naked or sick or in prison, and did not take care of you?"*

> *Then he will answer them, "Truly I tell you, just as you did not do it to one of the least of these, you did not do it to me"* [25:45–46].

Jesus in fact can be called the "Supreme Hospitalitor," for he laid down his life for others. The writer's intention in Matthew 25 is to show the certainty of the end time and to answer the question of who will be judged as righteous. Persons who are hospitable to strangers are doing those deeds as if the other person were Jesus Christ himself.

In this passage, Jesus makes it clear that we are not to reject the needy stranger like the son of man who was rejected and crucified. The stranger is to be welcomed, accepted, fed, and clothed. Welcoming the stranger opens the door to building relationships and developing deeper communion with one another and with God.

Our relationships with others are transformed when we seriously consider the reality that we are encountering Christ in the other person. That should affect all of our relationships, every day of our lives. The same principle of hospitality gets reinforced in these additional New Testament passages:

- **Matthew 10:40–42** points out that those who welcome the disciples of Christ are in fact welcoming Christ himself. The passage goes on to say that "'whoever gives even a cup of cold water to one of these little ones in the name of a disciple—truly I tell you, none of these will lose their reward.'"

- **1 Peter 4:7–11** urges us to show love in all our relationships and to give evidence of hospitality. We are to "be hospitable to one another without complaining" [v.9].

- **Hebrews 13:1–2**, as pointed out in the preceding chapter, encourages us to show "hospitality to strangers, for by doing that some have entertained angels without knowing it."

Whether we think of encountering an angel in the stranger, as suggested in Hebrew 13, or the actual presence of Christ, as suggested in Matthew 25, there is no question about the importance placed on hospitality to the stranger.

Overview

Some common themes about biblical hospitality emerge from a review of the passages mentioned in this chapter and from other biblical texts.

1. Although "hospitality" is not always mentioned by name, it was part of the very fabric of the Hebrew and Christian people.

2. Abraham both depended on the hospitality of others when he was a sojourner and provided hospitality to other sojourners in his home.

3. Hospitality is often pictured as an expression of faith and of thankfulness to God who delivered his people when they were strangers in Egypt and sojourners in Canaan.

4. The obligation to hospitality was in fact taken for granted in New Testament times. It was never seen as optional.

5. By entertaining the stranger or sojourner, we open ourselves to the blessings of God.

6. Hospitality is both a practiced act and an attitude toward others. We are to be open and accepting to all because God has been open and accepting to us.

7. The shared table brings together host, stranger, and God. The Lord's Supper (or communion or eucharist, depending on the terminology of your tradition) reminds us of our bonds with one another and also reminds us of the need to show hospitality to others.

The Oakland Experience

> **Concept:** A rural congregation belonging to a denomination declining in membership experienced increased vitality and growth as a result of biblical hospitality. The same emphasis can work in any congregation.

If thinking about a congregation that has experienced rapid growth for you the mental image of a huge physical facility in the suburban part of a major metropolitan center, you are about to be disappointed. Those words do not describe the Oakland Church.

The Oakland congregation is located in an Ohio farming community. People there have access to urban centers, but you would not use the word urban or suburban to describe the church's location—you would use the word country or rural.

While most people would always have described the congregation as "friendly," there was nothing spectacular about the church's program of outreach. In fact evangelism had come to be a word with negative connotations for most in the church.

The congregation's denominational identity has likewise not been growth-oriented. The Oakland Church is part of the Church of the Brethren, a relatively small Anabaptist denomination, which experienced significant persecution in Europe. Evangelism and growth have never been central to the church's stated priorities or self-image. Like Mennonite churches and the Quakers, the denominational emphasis has generally been on peace-making, working for justice, and simple living. The core beliefs of the Church of the Brethren are very similar to those of mainline Protestant denominations such as the United Methodist Church, the United Church of Christ, the American Baptist Churches, the Episcopal Church, the Presbyterian Church U.S.A., and the Evangelical Lutheran Church. The Church of the Brethren is also similar to most of those denominations in having experienced significant membership decline in recent decades.

Those in the Oakland congregation who would come for a meeting on evangelism would generally do so with their feet dragging and were more likely to come if a potluck supper was part of the evening. The reservations about evangelism held by the people at Oakland have much in common with the reservations experienced by members of other denominations:

- Not feeling comfortable asking others if they are "saved." It feels awkward to make a transition from "Hi, how are you this evening?" to "Do you feel that you have the right kind of relationship with God? Do you feel assured of your salvation?"

- Anxiety over making "cold calls" on others. All people are busy, and many have difficulty getting the amount of time that they want to spend in their homes with other members of the household. Knocking at someone's door without invitation and expecting that person to be responsive to talk about salvation and the church never seemed realistic.

- Inability to feel good about the oversimplification of the faith embodied in approaches like the four spiritual laws and other strategies based on the "right answers" to questions people themselves may not even be asking.

- The fear of rejection which accompanies asking someone in the family, in the neighborhood, or at the workplace to visit one's church.

- Not recognizing the extent to which all people need the sense of belonging and community which is present in the church as the body of Christ.

From Negative Connotations to Positive Practices

Yet the Oakland congregation has enjoyed almost a decade of steady growth, which has necessitated the expansion of the physical facilities. What happened?

- A crusade or revival? No.

- A new housing development at the back door of the church? No.

- A new minister? No.

- A new denominational identity? No.

What transformed the Oakland Church's life and, as a result, its ability to attract and hold new members, was an emphasis on biblical hospitality. The process began as the pastor (Fred) and the pastoral supervisory group began reflecting on an article by Don Miller in the journal *Brethren Life and Thought*. Miller's words about hospitality had great impact on that group.

We realized that we had in fact been practicing some aspects of hospitality but had not identified it as such. The actions were simply an outgrowth of childhood experiences and instruction for some in the church. As we began to look at ways in which we had already practiced hospitality, we suspected that those practices were largely responsible for the strength of the congregation. We wanted to better understand what had been happening in our congregation and what the potential might be.

The Oakland Church conducted its own survey of why people had joined the congregation over the past ten years. Responses indicated that the warmth and acceptance of hospitality were what had caused people to unite with us. When asked to share what impressed them most about the congregation, people made responses like these:

- Friendliness.

- A willingness to work together.

- A sense of closeness amid diversity and a strong sense of being connected with one another.

- Everyone is important—each can be himself or herself and gain meaning from the church.

- An alive, committed, faithful fellowship.

35

- Expressions of positive faith by others and by the church as a whole.

- A family atmosphere that shows concern and support for all its members.

What would happen, we wondered, if we practiced hospitality on a more intentional basis? We had no reservations at all about this approach. Hospitality not only felt comfortable and nonmanipulative to us; it also was fun!

Elements of Hospitality in the Church

As we began to become systematic and intentional about hospitality, we learned a great deal from one another and from the new people who became involved in our congregation. The following elements have all been part of our experience:

- We have emphasized that we are practicing biblical hospitality, and the Bible has been the starting place for our self-understanding and study.

- We've taken training seriously. ‚While many of us have learned various aspects of hospitality during childhood and through adult experiences, the intentional practice of hospitality in the church requires understanding and practice. We offer classes or groups to train new people in the practice of hospitality, and we also have refresher opportunities.

- We give people assignments to practice different aspects of hospitality. Those assignments are an important part of learning the art of hospitality, and they are also important in being sure areas of hospitality are not neglected in the life of the church. The entire church needs to understand and practice hospitality toward one another, toward visitors, and toward persons in the community, but we also need to be sure people do not fall through the cracks. Specific assignments take care of that.

- We began at a relatively early stage in our emphasis on hospitality to see signs of the concept affecting congregational life. We began to see people lingering more after services. Congregation members were increasingly inviting friends and visitors to share meals. The volume of phone calls among members and visitors picked up dramatically. People began showing a special interest in the more fringe members of the congregation. Another important sign was a new attitude of acceptance toward those in the church who were not especially friendly!

• We had people prepared to invite visitors to their homes for lunch, an action which makes a lasting impression on those who come.

• We cultivated the art of listening as a part of the practice of hospitality. The deacons took several initiatives to encourage listening to visitors. We also learned to listen with more care to our inactive members, and we learned from them. The fact that we listened to the needs and concerns of visitors and inactives made them more open to hearing what we had to say.

• Classes and groups in the church began systematic strategies to reach out to those who had become inactive and to those who were potential members. What had been simply good intentions before began to become practiced outreach. While not every effort succeeded, the number that did was significant positive reinforcement for our efforts.

• In all areas of congregational life, we saw people interacting with one another in more accepting and caring ways. Evaluation and judgment began to be suspended. The starting assumption for people increasingly was that the stranger should be seen and accepted as potential friend rather than simply as an unknown.

• And yes, we certainly did experience numerical growth. During the initial three-month period of the hospitality emphasis for which we maintained records, we found Sunday school attendance went up by 36% in comparison to the same period the previous year and worship attendance went up 19%. Continued growth has caused us to add a worship service and to expand our physical facilities. And as this book goes to press, yet another expansion is underway.

The practice of hospitality has strengthened our faith community at Oakland Church in our understanding of our calling. One person in lay leadership commented: "There is definitely an obvious challenge to our congregation: it is that we are all ministers, that we are all called." While that concept had been known to the membership in previous years, the emphasis on hospitality is what made it become real in the hearts and minds of many members.

If people are to be open to the offer of salvation, they must first feel **accepted**, **affirmed**, and **welcomed** by those who are part of the body of Christ. The church needs to be an open, receptive, affirming community where Christ's reconciling love can break down the walls of fear and hostility, competition and rivalry, and concerns about punishments and rewards. Hospitality creates that atmosphere, and our Lord can work through us in the process.

The Church Growth Movement and Hospitality

Many congregations have learned from the church growth movement. That movement has challenged us to examine the reasons for growth and decline in our congregations and denominations. Hospitality is not a church growth strategy as such. One does not practice hospitality in order to make the church grow. The emphasis with hospitality is on the guest, not on the growth of the organization extending the hospitality and not even on the needs of the individual serving as host.

The church growth movement at its best has made us aware that outreach to others in the name of Christ is a central part of the work of the Christian community. Many of us had grown too complacent and had not thought about outreach unless our churches were beginning to hurt financially. Some of the styles of evangelism that have flowed from the church growth movement, however, have been aggressive, manipulative, and sometimes even degrading. The Scriptures give no support for approaches to outreach that manipulate others. Strategies for outreach which are manipulative not only are likely to fail but also are likely to cause people to resist future, healthier outreach efforts.

The church growth movement has often emphasized homogeneous groupings—helping the church grow by reaching out to people who are very much like ourselves. That is a strategy which has been especially effective in some situations, and a massive body of data supports the reality that most people who visit a church do so because a family member, friend, coworker, or neighbor invited them. Obviously we are most likely to interact with and to invite persons who are very much like ourselves.

The homogeneous orientation, however, has also been a limiting factor for many congregations. This is especially true in situations in which the typical member of the congregation is very different than in the neighborhood surrounding the church. Hospitality certainly doesn't reject those who are similar to us, but a person motivated by biblical hospitality intentionally reaches out to the stranger, to the one who is different.

In some of its forms, the church growth movement has sought to change people. Hospitality offers space for the guest where change can take place. **Hospitality does not require change before extending acceptance.** Thus hospitality stretches us and pushes us to see others more as Christ would—to recognize the presence of Christ even in those who are very different from ourselves.

As warned in the first chapter, there are dangers in hospitality:

- It may in fact put us in contact with people who make us feel uncomfortable. Viewing all strangers as potential friends makes us vulnerable.

- Some people have a built-in resistance to any program, and those persons may not feel differently about one that makes hospitality intentional.

- We may fail to link the call to hospitality with the call to discipleship. Accepting the stranger or any other

participant in the Christian community is not synonymous with condoning or accepting every aspect of
his or her lifestyle or behavior. Ultimately, we welcome the outsider to become our friend and walk with
us on the road of Christian obedience and maturity.

* Hospitality can bring into the church persons who
  have a different theological background than most in
  the congregation. When hospitality is warm and
  sincere, new people will sometimes overlook
  differences in belief because they so greatly enjoy
  being part of the community. In time, however, those
  differences may become unacceptable. The Oakland
  Church has had to deal with this reality and has
  learned to be careful to give an adequate orientation
  to the core beliefs of the church for those who are
  considering membership.

* Hospitality can certainly become ingrown, causing us
  to look inward to our own personal network of
  friends rather than outward to those Christ seeks to
  introduce into our lives. This has been a temptation
  in some traditions in which people have practiced
  exemplary hospitality but have restricted it to those
  already known or related to members of the
  congregation.

* Practicing hospitality can become artificial. If we let
  the emphasis shift to church growth as an end in
  itself, making hospitality just another program, the
  stranger will quickly perceive the self-serving nature of
  our embrace and withdraw from it.

Biblical hospitality, however, can push through those
dangers and claim the rewards that come in truly embracing not
only the friends we already have, but also the strangers God
sends into our lives as individuals and congregations.

What Motivates Us?

> **Concept:** The practice of hospitality won't trans-
> form your congregation if it is viewed as only one
> more in a series of programs to strengthen the
> church. The majority of the congregation must, at
> a fundamental level, come to feel that hospitality
> is a core part of our responsibility as Christians
> and come to share a vision of the congregation as
> a truly welcoming, affirming, accepting place.

- "But we've done everything we were asked to do. I don't see why the congregation isn't growing."

- "I went to our denomination's church growth workshop last week, but I don't expect it to make any difference. I've been to four of them in the last five years, and my church is still in decline."

- "I thought we did the right things. We started a new contemporary worship service, and we bought newspaper and radio advertisements. Everything has fallen flat. I feel like we wasted all our money and energy."

- "I went to a conference where the speaker told us that technology was the key to reaching people in this postmodern era. We've invested in what I think is a wonderful website for the church. We're using Power-Point with the sermon. We've even experimented with some television ads using the new identity line from our denomination. But none of these things have made any difference that I can see."

The above speakers have all experienced the frustration of trying to achieve congregational growth without obtaining any clear results. Books have been written, workshops have been held, consultations have been available, and denominational programs have been attempted. Some of us have had at least brief periods of "church growth addiction," during which we've read, signed up for, or promoted every church growth strategy that came our way—or at least it's felt like that to us.

But in spite of all that energy, time, and money having been expended, many congregations are still not growing. Many that are growing are nevertheless failing to assimilate new persons as readily as they would like.

People can read the right books and attend the right events and still remain unmotivated to make the basic changes needed to become channels through which the lives of people and the life of the congregation can be transformed. Some people may say that they want new members, but when priorities must be set, they want their own needs put first. While we believe that hospitality is at the core of the change needed in a great many congregations, we also recognize that none of us can force people to do what they do not want to do. Shifts in attitude and vision are necessary to bring about increased church vitality and congregational growth.

The Necessity of Changing Attitudes

Creating a truly welcoming congregation is not just a matter of developing new brochures and creating a website. Brochures and websites can be a help in getting the attention of people and in interpreting what the church believes and does. They are rarely responsible for someone visiting a church and **never** responsible for someone continuing to attend and ultimately joining the congregation. Brochures are most useful when handed by one person to another along with an invitation to attend. Websites are a valuable ministry tool within the congregation and may catch the attention of people who are actively searching for a new church home. The best website in the world is not likely to gain the attention of someone who is not already seeking a deeper faith or a church connection.

The pie chart on the next page shows the top reason given by people for their decision to visit a particular congregation for the first time. As you can see, the influence of websites and of radio and television advertising is not very large. While factors such as the pastor's influence and the Sunday school account for some first-time visitors, the majority chooses to come because a family member, a friend, a coworker, or a neighbor invited them to do so. No matter how many books a person reads on church growth or how many seminars are attended, the main way to impact the numbers of people visiting a particular local congregation is by asking people to attend! That's how it happens!

% of People Who Visit a Church Because Of

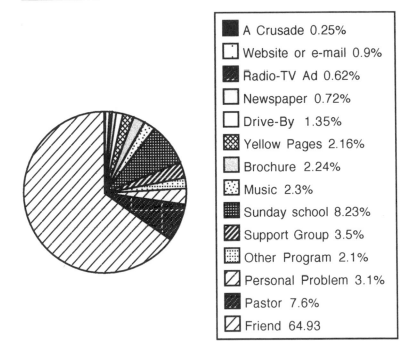

- ■ A Crusade 0.25%
- ☐ Website or e-mail 0.9%
- ▨ Radio-TV Ad 0.62%
- ☐ Newspaper 0.72%
- ☐ Drive-By 1.35%
- ▨ Yellow Pages 2.16%
- ▨ Brochure 2.24%
- ▨ Music 2.3%
- ▦ Sunday school 8.23%
- ▨ Support Group 3.5%
- ▨ Other Program 2.1%
- ▨ Personal Problem 3.1%
- ■ Pastor 7.6%
- ▨ Friend 64.93

LifeQuest research project

The influence of the pastor, of course, is of a personal nature. Those who cited a support group or another program did so in part because of the quality of interaction with other persons that took place through that program. Those who attended because of the music or the Sunday school have generally learned about the quality of those programs through other people. The quality of the interaction of church members and constituents with their family members, friends, coworkers, and neighbors and the willingness of church members to offer the hospitality of the congregation are by an overwhelming margin the major determining factors in people visiting a congregation.

Some persons maintain that the influence of television advertising for some large congregations is now passing that of one-to-one connection with people in bringing visitors to the church. While that may be true in some isolated instances, the message of national surveys through 2003 continues to be that person-to-person interaction is still the major factor for most congregations.

When a similar survey was conducted in 1995, church websites were not even offered as an option to those responding. The percentage of persons motivated to come for the first time by a website in the 2002 and 2003 research on which the above chart is based stands at only 0.9%. That is, however, a greater influence than crusades and a greater influence than radio, television, or newspaper advertising.

Our assumption is that increasing numbers of persons actively searching for a new church home will look at websites for information. But a church website, like the yellow pages which such sites may one day replace as a source of initial information, is never going to have much impact on persons not actively seeking information on potential church homes. It is not likely that websites will ever influence more than a small percentage of persons to come to a church for the first time. Their primary impact will be on providing valuable information about the congregation for persons who learn about it from another source—such as a friend, family member, neighbor, or coworker.

But what happens once a person visits the congregation? Even if the initial visit comes because of a website or a television advertisement, people generally do not continue coming unless the quality of what they experience in the congregation is very high. That includes the quality of congregational warmth or the perceived hospitality of the church.

The chart below shares the results of a 2003 and 2004 study in which persons who returned as visitors three or more times were asked to name the top three reasons for their continuing to return. The chart shows by bars the percentage of persons who named each factor as one of the three major influences on the decision to return.

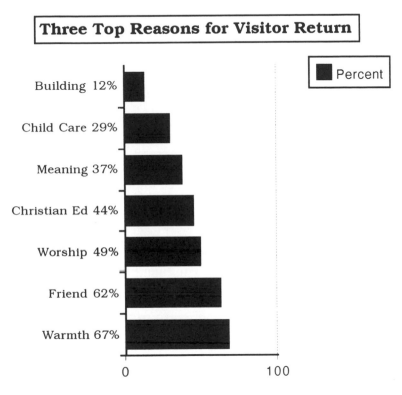

LifeQuest research project

Those asked to respond most commonly described their reasons for returning in words similar to these:

- "Because of the warmth of the welcome the congregation extended to me."

- "Because I have a friend in the congregation or made a friend during my visits."

- "Because the quality of the worship service helped me grow closer to God."

- "Because the quality of the Sunday school helped me or my child grow closer to God." (Sunday school, Wednesday night program, small group ministry, or other Christian education program)

- "Because my experiences there helped me in my search for meaning in life and a closer relationship with Christ."

- "Because the child care offered was excellent, and I felt good about having my child in nursery and/or Sunday school."

- "Because the building is such a marvelous facility with many opportunities."

In addition to the reasons in the chart, people named a wide range of other factors including the variety of programs and the opportunities for service. The top two reasons (warmth and friendship), however, both relate to the quality of interaction with those persons already in the congregation. Thus those participating in a study of hospitality, including those holding this book in their hands at this moment in time, need to remember that we are not simply talking about a change in program or strategy. **We are talking about a fundamental change in attitude toward those outside the church and toward those who come to the church as guests.**

When faced with one who is not known or with one whose religious connections are not known, our immediate response needs to be one of acceptance and warmth rather than of evaluation. When others bring their friends to church with them, our response on meeting them needs to be one of acceptance and warmth. Like Abraham to the three unexpected visitors at the entrance to his tent, we need to (figuratively speaking in our culture) bow to show our honor at their presence and then offer to them the very best that we have (whether that is sharing a meal or sharing in a Sunday school class). We need a vision of the church as a truly welcoming, accepting, and affirming center and to see ourselves as extensions of the body of Christ.

46

The Place of Vision

In his insightful book *Sacred Cows Make Gourmet Burgers*, Bill Easum warns us that:

> *Failure to build a shared vision is the biggest mistake that gifted leaders can make* [p. 83].

The purpose of this book and the journey we are taking together isn't to travel back to the Ancient Near East so that we can literally duplicate what happened there. We don't normally bow to others as a sign of greeting. We don't slaughter calves for our dinner guests. Most of us don't see what happens to our food before it hits the shelf in the grocery store, and some of us are opposed to eating veal. Others of us are opposed to eating any meat at all.

We don't want to return to the Ancient Near East. We do want to bring the essence, the vision of gracious hospitality of the Ancient Near East and of our Lord and Savior, to our own time, our own lives, and our own congregations. We do not want any guest to feel uncertainty in our presence. We also do not want a friend of ours to feel anxiety about acceptance from the rest of the church. We want:

- To show the honor and respect that was embodied in the bow of the Ancient Near East by our words and our warmth.

- To offer the fullest possible hospitality, including invitations to share in meals and to meet other persons in the household of faith.

- To reserve all judgment—and work on the assumption that the one who comes is a potential friend whose involvement will enrich our lives.

In the familiar Parable of the Good Samaritan, **Luke 10:25–37**, nothing is said about the worthiness of the person who was injured. No questions are raised about whether or not the injured party might have started the conflict or might have been drunk or on drugs. The parable also does not talk about

47

"correct" theological beliefs. The starting point for the Samaritan is one of acceptance and compassion. The behavior of the individual in need is not being evaluated. The priest, the Levite, and the Samaritan are the ones whose behavior is evaluated—and only one of the three has acted in an acceptable way as far as our Lord is concerned.

Think back to the other biblical passages shared in the second chapter. Again and again, we find that the behavior of the host is under evaluation, not the behavior of the guest. We are expected to provide warm, caring, welcoming environments to those who seek us out and to those we invite to share with us.

If this study is going to be fruitful for you and for any others who share with you, then it becomes of great importance to begin working on a vision of what it means for your church to become a place of true hospitality. Can you picture it in your mind? What does that mean for your physical facilities? What does that mean for the initial greeting people receive? What would you want to experience if you came to your congregation as a guest? You may want to visit some other congregations to experience what it is like to be a guest.

Mystery and Curiosity

Are we frightened or intrigued by the world? Do the differences that exist between ourselves and others constitute a source of anxiety or of fascination? If we have been clinging to a world view filled with foreboding, then embracing others within the church and within the broader society will be a threatening experience for us.

In *Further Along the Road Less Traveled*, popular author and psychiatrist Scott Peck shares this perspective on the place of curiosity in a mentally healthy life:

> *One of the things that characterize the most mentally healthy among us is their great taste for mystery and their profound curiosity. They are curious about*

everything: about quasars and lasers and schiz-
ophrenics and praying mantises and stars.
Everything turns them on [p. 77].

Jesus spoke of becoming like a little child to enter the
kingdom of heaven. As we all know and experience, one of the
major characteristics of children is their profound curiosity
about everything.

Why....? Why....? Why....?

We need to learn from children how to recapture a fascination
with life and with the people whose paths cross ours. Our
questions as adults should reflect genuine interest rather than a
probing and evaluating attitude. We need to see fascinating,
good possibilities in the stranger and also in the friend with
whom we may begin interacting in a different way by extending
an invitation to church.

The Place of Training

Unlike the case with some church growth strategies, most
people feel good about the concept of hospitality and about
learning to extend it to others. Most of us want to be welcoming. The majority of us, in fact, think we already are
welcoming! But most of us, in truth, need to improve. *And we
need to see that hospitality is not just another program—it
is in fact the very essence of the life and witness of the
Christian community.* When a church embodies that kind of
hospitality, people want to be part of it. Biblical hospitality
begins in the heart of each person.

During the years since the first edition of this book, both of
us have been involved in many consultations with congregations and with many judicatory workshops on hospitality. Steve
Clapp and others in the Christian Community organization have
conducted strategic planning surveys for hundreds of congregations, and those surveys include many items related to
hospitality. Almost without exception, we find that the level of
hospitality in congregations is not as great as leaders perceive it
to be. And true hospitality goes far beyond the initial smile and
handshake extended to a visitor on Sunday morning.

If you are reading this book as part of a study in which you are sharing with other persons, then you are already well on your way to the creation of a more hospitable congregation. If you are reading this book independently and want to begin making a difference in your congregation, one of the most valuable steps you can take is to get others involved in a study with you, so that they are exposed to the same chapters you are experiencing and so that you can work together on the vision of a church which practices great hospitality.

Experiencing Hospitality In the Church

Concept: The caring host provides the kind of acceptance and the opportunities that respond to the needs and comfort level of the guest.

Although she had spent all of her life in Charleston, South Carolina, Madeline moved to Phoenix, Arizona, following the death of her husband in a tragic automobile accident. She had seen an opening posted on her company's bulletin board for a position in the Phoenix office, and the idea of moving so far away from all the reminders of her husband felt like a good step to her. She was thirty-seven years old and had no children.

When she moved into an apartment complex in Phoenix on an unbearably hot June day, a woman in a neighboring apartment helped her unload boxes from her sport utility vehicle and in the process invited her to attend church on Sunday. That was quite a suggestion for Madeline, who had not darkened a church door since her wedding and had attended only a few times during her childhood and teenage years. Her life, however, felt out of balance, and she thought church might provide her what was needed.

She liked the neighbor who had pitched in so readily to help and wondered if there were more people like her in the congregation. She was horribly afraid of saying something foolish or doing something wrong since she had so little church background. Her neighbor had told her that it was perfectly acceptable to wear shorts to that congregation in the summer. Shorts in church? That sure didn't sound like the churches back home. She wondered what else would be different.

Brad and Ann moved to Phoenix at almost exactly the same time as Madeline. They were both in their mid-forties and had a seventh-grade daughter, a high school sophomore son, and a daughter who had just finished her freshman year of college. Their dog, cat, and goldfish also made the trip, though there were a few goldfish casualties along the way. Brad and Ann had both taken new positions in Phoenix and were excited about the transition. They had lived in Portland, Oregon, for many years but had always appreciated everything in Phoenix on their vacations there—except the summer heat. Both of their new positions represented significant advancements, and they were thrilled with the 4,000 square foot home that they had been able to buy.

They had been very active in a congregation in Portland for the past ten years, and their pastor had already made contact with a church of the same denomination in Phoenix. They were hoping it would have as strong a youth program for their two younger children as they had enjoyed in Portland. Brad thought it would feel a little strange to be coming into a church as an outsider when he had just finished a three-year term as the chairperson of the church board in Portland.

Eddie arrived in Phoenix on the same day as Madeline, but instead of moving into an apartment by himself, he was sharing a somewhat run-down apartment with three other men. Eddie had just been released from a Federal Correctional Institution where he had served a five-year sentence on a drug charge. He was twenty-seven years old and had not finished high school. He had gotten a G.E.D. while in prison but felt that he had learned relatively little in the process. Eddie was determined to get his life in order, and the chaplain in prison had helped him reclaim his faith in Christ. He had a lot of bitterness over the length of his sentence, but he wanted very much to prove that the judge had been wrong about his potential for good.

Eddie had lived in Tucson before his arrest, but he had no desire to return to his old circle of friends in that city. He knew he would have to be careful not to resume his drug habit or to develop a problem with alcohol, which had really been his drug of choice until the time in prison. He had a job at a fast food restaurant and planned to enroll in a local community college. He had not belonged to a church before, but following his imprisonment, he wanted to become active in one. In fact he had promised the chaplain that he would be in church the first Sunday he was in Phoenix. He made arrangements to borrow a car for Sunday morning from one of the others in the apartment. Eddie decided to try a congregation that ran an advertisement in the newspaper, which said:

> *All people are welcome here.*
> *Your past no longer matters.*
> *The present and future are*
> *what matter to us and to God.*
> *Come share with us.*

That sounded like the kind of place Eddie needed. It also happened to be the same church that Madeline and Brad, Ann, and their children visited that Sunday.

In the Shoes of Others

What a challenge and what an opportunity for a local congregation! Think about the needs the visitors just described have in common and also about the unique backgrounds they bring to the congregation. They have in common:

- The fact that they've all just moved to Phoenix from other places and have never lived in that city before.

- The fact that they all want to feel accepted in the new congregation.

- The fact that this particular congregation may be considerably more casual than they've experienced in the past.

- The fact that they all will be interested in developing new friendships with people.

But they also bring unique needs and may well respond in different ways to what happens on Sunday morning. For example:

- Madeline has to decide how quickly she wants to let people she meets in the church know that her husband died recently. She wants to be open with people, but she also feels like his death is still far too painful a topic for conversation.

53

- Madeline has no interest in dating. She feels that she will need a lot of time before having any interest in that kind of social life.

- Eddie doesn't want to date for a couple of months, but he is already looking forward to doing so.

- Madeline and Eddie both have had almost no past experience in congregational life. They feel uneasy about everything and are quite afraid of looking foolish to others. Neither of them feels sure about what happens in Sunday school. Madeline's neighbor has invited her to attend a class with her, but Madeline is a little uneasy about that. Eddie just plans to go to the worship service. His reading skills aren't good, and he fears that people may have to read aloud from the Bible in the Sunday school classes.

- Brad and Ann have had years of experience in the life of the church and are staying in the same denomination. While there will no doubt be some differences, they already have a good idea what to expect. They want to become involved as quickly as possible. Brad hopes it will be possible to arrange lunch with the pastor that week.

- Madeline no doubt still has a lot of grief work to do. A setting which will let her share when she feels ready to do so would be worth a great deal to her.

- Eddie feels lost about what to say to people about the years immediately preceding his move to Phoenix. How will people in the church respond to him if he shares that he's spent the last five years in prison? He wants to be honest with people, but he also wants to be accepted. He likes the saying of the church in the newspaper, but he also has to wonder if that's true or just advertising copy.

- Eddie has a very low income and is likely to continue having a low income for several years to come. Even a tithe of his income to the church won't be a lot, and he won't have much money to participate in church social activities.

• Brad and Ann are in a position to give substantial financial support to the congregation. Having served as board chairperson in Portland, Brad wonders things like what it costs to air condition the facility in Phoenix, what the pastor and other staff are paid in comparison to Portland, and how financially healthy the church is.

• Madeline is the only one of them who already knows someone in the congregation. She has the option of going to church with her neighbor if she wants to attend both Sunday school and worship, or she can simply meet her neighbor at one of the church entrances for worship.

When we think about hospitality, it's important for us to keep in mind just how different the needs of people can be and how different their levels of comfort in church can be. Church members are likely to differ in their own feelings about these visitors.

Any pastor and most church members rejoice to have people like Brad, Ann, and their children move into the community and immediately come to church. Most people will feel sorry for Madeline once they learn about her situation, and single males who meet her are likely to be frustrated that she has no interest in dating. Some persons will feel sorry for Eddie when they learn about his situation, but there will be others who are afraid of him and will wonder if he would ever bring a young person in the church into contact with drugs.

How would your congregation respond to the persons just described? These are all real people, and they all visited the same Phoenix congregation on the same day. We'll share more about the response to them later in the chapter.

From the standpoint of biblical hospitality, the church has the same obligation to be a gracious, affirming host to Eddie, to Madeline, and to Brad, Ann, and their children. There's a basic level of acceptance and affirmation that all these visitors should receive. As time passes, whether or not these persons continue to feel accepted will depend in part on the extent to which people in the church can respond to their various needs and levels of comfort with congregational life.

55

Think again about the definitions of hospitality that were shared in the first chapter.

Hospitality is the **attitude** and **practice** of providing the **atmosphere** and **opportunities**, however risky, in which strangers are free to become friends, thereby feeling accepted, included, and loved. The relationship thus opens up the possibility for eventual communion among the host, the stranger, and God.

Hospitality involves recognizing the presence of Christ in family, friends, coworkers, neighbors, and complete strangers. It means responding to others as we would respond to the presence of Christ in our midst.

Some other words from the Ancient Near East and from Scripture may be helpful in thinking about the different situations represented within a congregation:

The **foreigner** referred most often to a person who made contact with Israel as a trader, traveler, or soldier. This individual would generally not cut ties with the original home.

An **alien** was differentiated from the foreigner and was a permanent resident of the community. Anyone not related by blood to a particular tribe or clan but permanently associated with it was considered an alien.

The **sojourner** lived in the community and had responsibilities, but the community was not fully his or her own. The sojourner's residence was temporary, and a return to the permanent home would eventually come.

Thinking about Eddie, Madeline, and Brad, Ann, and their children makes us aware of the differences in their comfort levels and their needs from the congregation. Now think about the needs, comfort levels, and expectations of persons in the following categories in terms of contact with your church. How do you and the church respond to:

- The person who is present every week and who has several close friends in the church? (This probably describes most people reading this book!)

- The person who is regular in attendance but whose closest friends are outside of the congregation?

- The person who attends only on an occasional basis and doesn't feel tightly bonded to the congregation?

- The person who has become chronically inactive and rarely attends?

- The guest who already knows several members?

- The guest who knows almost no one in the congregation except the person who extended the invitation to come?

- The guest who has just moved to the area and truly knows no one in the congregation?

From the standpoint of biblical hospitality, we want as individuals and as congregations to make the warmest possible response to all those with whom we come in contact.

Appreciating Variation in Comfort Zones

A couple attended the Oakland congregation for many weeks without anyone in the church getting an opportunity to visit with them or even to learn their names. Their normal pattern was to arrive just as the service was beginning and to sit at the back of the sanctuary, as close to the door as possible. When the last hymn came, they were out of their seats and out of the door before there was any possibility of Fred or anyone else greeting them.

While respectful of people's differences in comfort zones, Fred likes greeting everyone, and his curiosity about the couple became overwhelming. He finally made arrangements to leave the chancel area early one Sunday and went out of the church through a side door. When he reached the door through which the couple always left, Fred found they were already out and running! He ran too and managed to extend a brief welcome (and good-bye!) to them. He was not, however, successful in getting their names before they left.

But they kept coming! They eventually stayed through the benediction and gave their name, but that was six months after they had started attending. Few people will wait that long to reveal their names, but some people are very slow to make commitments to Christ and the church.

Most people experience moderate anxiety when going into a new setting and meeting new persons. A minority of persons in North America, between 3% and 9% (depending on the study), experience significant anxiety when they are with large groups of people and are initially very uncomfortable being introduced to others and interacting with others. Guests who habitually leave the worship service before the benediction or closing prayer may be persons whose anxiety levels in group settings are especially high and who need to avoid interaction until they have grown far more comfortable.

In Phoenix, Madeline elected not to go to the Sunday school class with her neighbor, Sue, but she did go to church. Sue met her at a side door before the second worship service and sat with her in the sanctuary. Afterwards Sue introduced Madeline to four people (one married couple and two single people) who were members of the Sunday school class. Madeline was struck not only by how pleasant the people were but also by the fact that they did not pry. She volunteered that she had lived in Charleston for many years, and she found herself in an animated conversation with the couple who had both grown up in Atlanta and had visited Charleston on many occasions.

No one said anything to her that made her feel she needed to say something about her husband's death. Most of the conversation focused on life in Phoenix and the positive feelings the people had about the church staff and the rest of the congregation. Sue and the couple who had grown up in Atlanta talked about the possibility of having brunch together and invited Madeline to join them. Madeline felt comfortable accepting the invitation, and the four of them visited at the restaurant for such a long time that the manager finally asked if they could leave so the restaurant could be closed until the evening meal. During that lengthy conversation, Madeline did find herself telling them about her husband's death.

Madeline liked the fact that Sue introduced her to the married couple and to two other single people. Because of the circumstances that had made her single, she felt more comfortable in some ways with people who were married. She also appreciated the fact that Sue had not shared with the others the things that Madeline had confided in her during the unpacking process.

Brad, Ann, and their children also had a good first experience with the congregation. They arrived for Sunday school and all went to their respective classes. A couple in the class Brad and Ann attended introduced them to the senior pastor and the associate pastor during the fellowship time between Sunday school and the second worship service. Both the senior pastor and the associate pastor had known that Brad and Ann would be arriving soon because of the contact made with the church by the Portland pastor, and they were delighted to meet them. The senior pastor and Brad scheduled a lunch together. The associate pastor introduced Ann to the education chairperson who was immediately interested in all the years Ann had devoted to teaching and to training teachers. The two of them made plans for lunch during the week.

When they got into their car at the end of the morning, Brad immediately grabbed his small notebook out of the glove compartment and started making notes of all the people they had met. He and Ann were already starting to feel like they belonged. A couple in the Sunday school class with two high school age children had invited them to go out for brunch together after church, but Brad and Ann had decided to take a raincheck because their high school son appeared a little overwhelmed by the morning.

And he was in fact overwhelmed. He had met a lot of people his age in the high school class, but he felt like it was going to be hard to fit in with the others, who all seemed to be so close to each other. The seventh-grade daughter was enthusiastic about the other young people in her Sunday school class and was looking forward to the junior high youth group on Wednesday evening. The college daughter had attended a young singles class, which she had thoroughly enjoyed except for the fact that it had twice as many females as males!

That afternoon, one of the senior high youth group advisors telephoned their high school son to extend an invitation to the Youth Supper and Forum that evening. The advisor offered to have one of the senior highs come by to pick him up, but the son decided to drive himself, so he would feel like he could slip away early if he didn't enjoy the group. He in fact did enjoy the group.

Eddie was the one with the most misgivings about going to church, and he was the one who had the most mixed feelings at the end of the morning. Several people did greet him. He talked about being from Tucson, being new in town, and wanting to take some community college courses. One of those who greeted Eddie escorted him to a young man in his early twenties who was enrolled in a community college. They had a short visit, during which Eddie felt awkward. The visit was terminated by the young man's desire to say good-bye to the attractive visitor who had just moved from Portland with her parents!

While Eddie did not visit with anyone who shared a brunch invitation, he was surprised by two phone calls during the week. An elderly couple he had met phoned to say they had really enjoyed meeting him and wanted him to come to supper some night that week. Because he had to work every evening that week, Eddie had to decline, but he accepted their invitation to join them for brunch the following Sunday. Then he received a phone call from the senior pastor who asked if Eddie would be free to join him for breakfast or lunch sometime the following week. Eddie accepted the invitation and was more than a little surprised that the senior pastor of this rather large congregation would take the time to share a meal with someone so young and whose clothes were out of style.

The couple, both in their seventies, who had brunch with him the next week, made a real difference in his life. Eddie had been determined not to tell anyone about having been in prison. To his surprise, however, the couple shared as they were visiting that they had a grandson who was having so many problems with alcohol that they feared he would get into trouble with the law. It was clear that they still loved and respected the grandson, and Eddie found himself telling them about his own experiences with alcohol, drugs, and prison. At the end of the meal, they both hugged him and scheduled another time to eat together. Then he found himself sharing the story with the senior pastor, who shocked him by saying how much he respected him for what he was doing to turn his life around.

The congregation described did not handle everything perfectly. The college student to whom Eddie was introduced obviously abandoned that conversation too quickly. That was at least in part responsible for Eddie leaving the church with mixed feelings.

The class for Brad and Ann's high school son didn't succeed in making him feel completely comfortable the first time he attended. In fact, there may not have been anything the high school class could have done which would have made him feel completely at ease. The transition from one community to another and from one church to another is a major one and is especially difficult for someone who has already started high school.

The follow-up of the elderly couple and of the senior pastor to Eddie more than compensated for the hasty conversation with the other college student. Brad and Ann's son was mentioned to the youth group advisor who called him that same afternoon. All of these actions were respectful of the comfort zones the visitors had.

Creating Places for People To Belong

But what happens after those new members have been coming for a few weeks? Their continued experience of welcome in the congregation depends in part on their becoming involved in small groups and developing friendships. A good beginning has already happened for the particular persons discussed:

- Brad and Ann and their children have all started attending Sunday school classes. Their junior high daughter and senior high son have both been invited to evening youth groups.

- Madeline didn't attend the Sunday school class, but now that she has met four people in it as well as Sue, she will probably start attending.

*   Eddie is the one not yet pulled into a class or a small group. His initial bonds in the congregation are in fact to the elderly couple and to the senior pastor. These are solid bonds, but in time he also needs to be part of a group or class that has more persons in his own age bracket.

Some congregations are dependent on a multitude of different groups and classes for the integration of new people. Such churches often have men's groups, women's groups, Sunday school classes, Bible study groups, prayer groups, task forces, short-term study groups, musical groups, and more.

A growing number of congregations are organizing the church around a total small group emphasis and involve every active person in a cell group. Cell groups then become a foundational unit of the congregation. When someone new visits the church, one of the first steps in assimilation is to start that person in a small group.

In the Oakland Church, every effort is made to get a visitor into a small group or other educational opportunity within three weeks of the first visit. This helps people begin to build solid relationships with others and can also be an aid to them in working through faith issues.

Welcoming Strangers

Concept: While our culture teaches us to fear strangers, we also know that our best friends were once strangers to us. Life is transformed when we see the stranger as a potential friend.

We've all received and extended advice about strangers. Most of that counsel consists of admonitions to protect ourselves and others from the harmful influence or actions of those who are unknown to us. We are especially concerned about teaching our children to live safely. Statements and accounts like the following are commonplace:

- "Don't accept a ride from a stranger."

- "Don't go to the bathroom alone at the movies."

- "Don't accept gifts from strangers."

- "Don't take candy from someone you don't know."

- "Be careful of people who look like. . . . You can never be sure what someone like that will do."

- "Did you hear what happened to that man who stopped to help a person who had a flat tire?"

- "Did you hear what happened to that woman who let the stranger into her house?"

- "It probably doesn't mean anything, but I just had such an uneasy feeling when I met him."

As shared earlier in this book, we know that the world in which we live is not a safe one. Much of the advice contained in the preceding quotations is especially relevant for children. Yet we must be careful that we don't instill too deep a fear in our children and teenagers, and we need to avoid the trap of living in fear ourselves.

Our View of the Home

How we view our homes correlates to an extent with our attitudes toward strangers:

• Do you see your home as a castle with a moat around it and towers from which you can defend your property and those who live there?

• Do you see your home as a gathering place? Do you like to entertain?

• Do you see your home as a get-away or an escape from the pressures of life? Do you want to avoid bringing problems or controversy into the home?

• Do you see your home as a continuing work of art? Do you take great pride in the design, the furnishing, and the cleanliness of your home? Do you find yourself feeling resentful when other people are in your home, or do you covet opportunities to show people what you've accomplished?

• Do you see your home as Grand Central Station with lots of people passing through all the time—some of whom you know well and some not at all well?

An image of the home as Grand Central Station or as a gathering place tends to make us more receptive to strangers, whether we encounter those strangers in the workplace, the neighborhood, the grocery store, or the church. If your home seems like a castle or a get-away, you may be more cautious about encouraging people to call or visit you at home. Does that attitude extend to your relationships outside of the home?

There's nothing wrong with the attitudes toward the home just expressed. Most of us have feelings about the home which shift depending on what is happening in our lives. After an extended period of the home as Grand Central Station, we may start to develop great fondness for the home as get-away, though closing down Grand Central Station can be a tough job!

We need, however, to be sensitive to the reality that our attitudes toward strangers are formed by various influences:

- The things we've heard from other people.
- Accounts in the media.
- The way we feel about our homes and families.
- The experiences we've had.

Another influence may be how many good friends we already have. Someone who has just moved to a community finds everyone a stranger and is very conscious of the need to begin making new friends. Those of us who have lived in the same place for many years may already have so many friends that we don't feel a particular need for one more. We may wish we could figure out how to get more time with the friends we do have! Such an attitude, however, closes us to what we might gain from new friendships—and especially from friendships with persons who are different from us in significant ways. We may miss some of the blessings God seeks to share with us through new relationships.

The Essence of Hospitality

Our best friends were once strangers to us. There are valid reasons for wanting our homes to feel insular and safe, but those efforts do not always have the desired effect. By avoiding or locking out the stranger, we may in fact be locking out the blessings of God:

> *Do not neglect to show hospitality to strangers, for by doing that some have entertained angels without knowing it.*
> **Hebrews 13:2**

Hospitality to the stranger is assumed throughout the Old and New Testament Scriptures. Again and again, as in the Parable of the Good Samaritan, the questioning is not on the worthiness of the stranger but on the faithfulness of the one encountering the stranger. The Samaritan did not ask of the man who was injured: "Did you bring this on yourself? Were you trying to do a drug deal? Why weren't you traveling with someone else for safety?" The Samaritan simply responded to the human need that was encountered. The priest and the Levite who passed by are the ones whose behavior is called into question by our Lord's telling of the parable. Look once more at the core definitions of this book:

> **Hospitality** is the **attitude** and **practice** of providing the **atmosphere** and **opportunities**, however risky, in which strangers are free to become friends, thereby feeling accepted, included, and loved. The relationship thus opens up the possibility for eventual communion among the host, the stranger, and God.
>
> **Hospitality** involves recognizing the presence of Christ in family, friends, coworkers, neighbors, and complete strangers. It means responding to others as we would respond to the presence of Christ in our midst.

Whether we start with the assumption that the unknown person will be an enemy or a friend makes a difference! When anyone comes to our church or shows an interest in religious concerns, our starting assumption certainly should be that such a person shares with us a pull toward the heart of God. Such a person is a potential friend, perhaps sent to us by God for the enrichment of our lives.

Think how your view of the new person in your neighborhood, your office, or the church would be transformed if your starting assumption was:

> *This is a person sent by God who may be a great blessing to my life, or this is a person sent by God in order for me to be a blessing to his or her life.*

Obviously such blessings have a tendency to flow in both directions! How can we best show hospitality in the church?

What We Want When We Are Strangers

There are some important things which most of us want to experience when we are in the position of strangers, especially in terms of the church. Reflect on what it would be like to be a visitor to your congregation. Read this list carefully, and place a check beside those items that need more attention by yourself or by your church in order to provide a more welcoming setting:

_____ When visiting a church, most people don't want to be ignored. People expect those who are sitting near them to share brief introductions before or after the service, Sunday school class, or small group.

_____ When visiting a church, almost no one wants to be overwhelmed. Two-thirds of those who visit congregations for the first time do **not** want to be introduced in worship to the whole congregation. They prefer meeting people on a one-to-one basis. Introduce the new person to a few other people— not to every single person whose attention you can get.

_____ People especially do not want to feel ignored during a designated fellowship time. If they go to a gathering spot for coffee and donuts, they assume that some people will visit with them. They will feel rejected if church members are all in tight groups with people they already know. Be alert during such times for people who are standing alone.

_____ Visitors generally appreciate name tags for themselves and for the members of the church. That makes it easier to remember names and avoids awkwardness over names not being heard correctly the first time shared. Remember that you as a member only have the name of one new person to learn; the visitor has dozens or hundreds of names to eventually learn if he or she joins the church.

67

Name tags can also make it easier for you to introduce the new person to others in the church, whose names may not be as familiar as you would like!

    People don't want to feel as though they are being required to pass an entrance exam. Most will feel resentful of conversations which make it appear that someone is attempting to do research on family background and church activity. Churches with a strong ethnic membership, such as those with many descendants from Sweden or Germany, for example, sometimes act as though those people who have last names that sound a certain way are more acceptable than others.

Remember that in the Ancient Near East, the name of the guest was not even asked until after a meal had been shared. While we exchange names at a much earlier time in our culture, we need to be careful that the process of doing so does not cause us to act as though the name makes more difference than it should.

    Some people are anxious about how others will respond to certain aspects of their background. A person may be divorced, a single parent who has never married, unemployed, an alcoholic, or an ex-convict. These are not pieces of information they may want to share in initial conversations.

We do not want in an initial conversation to push someone to fill in the gaps in his or her history. When we see an adult with a child, we should not immediately move to a question like: "Where is your husband?" or "Where is your wife?" It's better to let the other person share family information as he or she wishes to do so.

    People want to feel that others are interested in them and pleased to have them present. They respond very well to genuine expressions of delight at their presence.

There are many topics of conversation that are good ones with people you've just met in the church:

- *Ask how that person happened to choose your church to visit.*

- *Share how you became involved in the church.*

- *Ask that person how he or she feels about living in your community.*

- *Say something about the weather—it's trite, but it works.*

- *Ask that person where he or she is originally from (just don't stay focused on the question as though it's of vital importance).*

- *Share something which you especially like about your church.*

- *Ask if the person has any questions about the church.*

____ Parents are always delighted when people show interest in their children. Direct part of your conversation to the child or teenager who is with the adult who is visiting. Compliment the child or teenager on his or her appearance.

____ If the person has an obvious physical disability, he or she will appreciate an offer of assistance if appropriate, such as information on elevator location for a person using a wheelchair or a walker. A person who is visually impaired or blind may need assistance in moving from one place to another. Beyond such clearly needed assistance, people with disabilities would generally prefer that conversation not center on the disability (thus making it appear that the disability is more important than the person).

____ People appreciate directions to the sanctuary, an appropriate Sunday school class, or a gathering place for refreshments.

____   ***People almost universally appreciate an invitation to share a meal either that day or at a mutually agreeable date later in the week. Few things show hospitality in a more meaningful way than having someone as your guest for a meal. Even if a person declines the initial invitation, the fact that it was given is still appreciated. Churches which focus on hospitality have a lot of people hosting others for meals.***

____   People appreciate being remembered with a phone call the week following their visit. It feels good to know that someone remembered you and took the time to call and reinforce how good it was to have you present. That can be an opportunity to extend an invitation to a meal, a Sunday school class, or another opportunity.

____   People appreciate returning the following week and finding that people to whom they were introduced remember them and are delighted to see them again.

____   People who are insecure about church involvement or who feel uncomfortable in large crowds appreciate sensitivity to their desire to go slowly in getting acquainted with others.

Estimates are that between 3% and 9% of the North American population experience significant discomfort in large crowds. What appears to be aloofness may in fact simply be an unavoidable response to a large group of people. Such persons will often respond better to a phone call or a visit during the week than to a lengthy discussion in the middle of a crowd on Sunday morning. Very few people who experience such anxiety in crowds ever talk about it with other people. We simply need to be sensitive to the possibility that this could explain the behavior of another person.

____   People appreciate literature about the church being shared with them. Brochures and newsletters can help answer questions at their leisure.

____ Young adults and teenagers who come as visitors are likely to dress somewhat more casually than some congregational members. A compliment to such a visitor about something he or she is wearing (assuming the compliment is sincerely meant!) is a good way to affirm that informal dress is fine in your church.

Of course it's possible that members of your church do not feel that informal dress is satisfactory. That's a position that many congregations, however, are rethinking. While churches in most parts of the country have not gone quite as casual as the Phoenix congregation mentioned in the last chapter in which shorts are worn by many people, a great many churches are moving toward more informal attire. There are two factors behind this trend.

First, a large number of workplaces have moved to more casual dress. That in turn has changed expectations about the weekend; people invest less money in suits, ties, and dress shoes.

Second, many young adults are increasingly dressing casually for all sorts of occasions. A survey of young adult males in 2003 showed that 38% did not own a suit or sport coat!

____ Strangers appreciate arrangements that make it easy for them to know how to find the church, where to park, where to enter the church, and where to find things in the church. Clear signs to the church, clearly marked parking, clearly marked entrances, and clearly posted signs and directions inside the church help.

That process can be made even warmer with a greeter in the parking lot and a greeter at each entrance for the Sunday school time as well as worship services. Oakland Church has utilized parking lot greeters for some time, and visitors have repeatedly expressed their appreciation for that early welcome. Some churches have parking places close to the main entrance reserved for visitors as a way of showing that visitors are honored guests.

_____ Visitors appreciate greeters and ushers who not only show warmth and genuine interest but who also have been trained to anticipate needs and to answer questions effectively. Ushers can often help by making an introduction to another person in the congregation.

Training for greeters and ushers is crucial. See the publication **The First Thirty Seconds: A Guide for Greeters and Ushers** *by Joan Hershey, listed in the* Resources and References *chapter at the end of this book.*

_____ Visitors appreciate announcements and the sharing of joys and concerns being done in a way which does not cause them to be excluded. That means the speaker should always give his or her name, instead of assuming everyone already knows him or her. That also means giving sufficient context for announcements, joys, and concerns so that they will make sense to a visitor. If a meeting or activity only involves a small number of people, probably no announcement should be made in worship.

_____ People appreciate instructions for the service being clearly stated by the worship leader or in the bulletin. Is communion open or closed? Do people come to the front of the church for communion? Are persons in the church sinners, debtors, or trespassers as far as the Lord's Prayer is concerned? Are words for all responses and songs available in the bulletin or a hymnal? Do not assume that guests will know the words to the *Gloria Patri* or the *Doxology*.

The next time you go to your church, make observations from the perspective of a guest to your congregation. You'll be surprised what a difference that makes in your view of the life of your church. You might also talk with some people who have recently visited your congregation and find out what they experienced.

Welcoming Children

Concept: Children belong as fully to the Christian community as do their parents. Our Lord always showed special consideration to children; we should do the same, which means looking at the life of the church from a child's perspective.

Jessica was seven years old and did not feel as enthusiastic about the move to Pennsylvania as the rest of her family. Her father was happy because the move from Michigan was the result of a significant promotion. Her mother was happy because the move put them only fifteen miles from her parents. Her younger sister was happy because Grandma and Grandpa would now be the ones providing child care; her older brother was happy because his new school had intramural soccer, computers in every classroom, and other opportunities that hadn't been available in the small school district in Michigan.

Jessica had never made friends quickly and being made to leave the few close friends she had developed seemed horribly unfair. The family cocker spaniel, Betsy, had died just before the move. The whole family had loved Betsy, but Jessica had always lavished the most attention on the dog, who had slept at the foot of her bed each night. Now she didn't have Betsy to listen to her and nuzzle her and reassure her.

When they pulled into the church parking lot on Sunday morning, Jessica felt overwhelmed by the rows and rows of cars and the huge building. Their last church had been very small, and they could walk to it from their house. She normally resisted holding her mother or father's hand when walking, but she put a vice grip on her mother's hand as they went into the church.

The greeters talked to her parents for what seemed to Jessica like a very long time and then spent more time making comments about her sister: "What a cute, darling, darling little girl. We're so glad to have you here. You're just as beautiful as your mother."

Then, almost as an afterthought, the woman who was doing the greeting patted Jessica on top of the head and said, "And what is the name of this darling little girl? We're so glad to have you here this morning too. What grade are you in school? How do you like living in Pennsylvania? Did you get that cute little dress somewhere here in Pennsylvania?" Jessica would have answered the questions, but the woman just kept on asking them without giving opportunity for any response. Jessica decided not to bother, and then heard, "Well, isn't she the shy one? Not wanting to talk to anybody yet. Well, that's all right. You'll talk when you have something to say, I'm sure."

I'll talk when you shut up, Jessica thought to herself. She would never say such a thing aloud. She tuned out everything around her and hardly even noticed that her mother walked her on down the hallway and into a classroom for second graders. The next thing she knew her mother was prying her fingers loose and leaving her alone in the room. She turned and started to follow her mother out of the room, but the teacher put a gentle hand on her shoulder and said, "Now, Jessica, you need to stay here with us. We're going to have a really good time, and you have a lot of other people to meet. My name is Martha, and I'm one of the teachers."

The door closed, and Jessica's heart sank as she could no longer see her mother. She turned toward the class and saw twenty children staring at her, most of them smiling. She wanted to run but had no idea where to go. "Marian," she heard the teacher say, "come here and meet our new friend."

Marian walked up to Jessica, gave her a big smile, and stuck out her hand. "Hi! I'm Marian, and I'm glad you came today."

"Jessica," the teacher explained, "Marian just started coming to our church about a year ago, and she didn't know any of us when she started. I thought she could be your special friend for the next few weeks and help you get acquainted with the others in the class."

And Jessica began to feel better. She met more people than she could remember, but she got to visit especially with Marian and three others as they worked together on a play about the Good Samaritan. Four other small groups were also working on plays based on parables, and Jessica had a good time. There were three teachers in the room, and both of the other teachers introduced themselves to her during the session.

By the time her mother and father came to get her at the end of the Sunday school class, Jessica felt a lot better. It still wasn't as nice as being in her old church where she knew everyone, but she thought Marian might be a really good friend. Marian wanted Jessica to come to her house during the week.

Jessica was careful, however, not to appear too pleased to her parents. She still was unhappy about the move, and she certainly didn't want them to think that she'd had a good time.

And she certainly did not have a good time during the worship service. The beginning of the worship service was just as boring as in her old church, and she didn't recognize any of the songs. Then her father made her join the other children who went to the front for the children's sermon.

The pastor had a nice smile, but he used a lot of words that Jessica couldn't understand. "Be saved. . . reconciliation. . . redemption. . ." and something about "the blood of the lamb." Jessica had no idea what lamb he was talking about, and she sure didn't know why she should be thankful for its blood. She didn't want to see any blood—the sight of it always made her sick. In fact sitting there thinking about this poor bloody lamb made her start to feel nauseous.

Thankfully she didn't faint or throw up. That would have been embarrassing. What happened next was as bad though. She found herself being herded along with the other children out a side door of the sanctuary and into a room where they had to stay for something called "Children's Church" while the rest of the worship service proceeded for her parents. She kept wondering if her parents would be able to find her in this huge church building. Maybe they wouldn't. It would have been better if Marian had still been with her, but Marian hadn't stayed for church. Jessica was almost overwhelmed with relief when her mother, father, and brother finally arrived. They picked her up before getting her little sister from the nursery, so that was nice.

75

"Well, wasn't that just wonderful?" her mother asked Jessica. "You got to leave that boring service and have your own time with others who are in grade school. Wasn't that nicer than having to sit through the whole service like we did before? Just think how many new friends you're going to make."

Her mother didn't get it. Her mother wasn't going to get it. "It was okay," Jessica reluctantly acknowledged. "But I really didn't like the kids who stayed for church as much as the ones in the Sunday school class. I'd rather be in Michigan."

"Well, you're not in Michigan, Jessica," her father firmly said. "As a matter of fact, I've had about enough of your saying that you'd rather be in Michigan. We're in Pennsylvania, and it's time you got used to it. Grow up."

Coming as Children

Grow up. We all do grow up, at least physically, but that doesn't necessarily mean we grow closer to God. Jesus placed great importance on children and wanted to be accessible to them. Consider these words from Matthew:

> *Then little children were being brought to him in order that he might lay his hands on them and pray. The disciples spoke sternly to those who brought them; but Jesus said, "Let the little children come to me, and do not stop them; for it is to such as these that the kingdom of heaven belongs." And he laid his hands on them and went on his way.*
> **Matthew 19:13–15**

The Gospel of Mark has a similar account, in which Jesus shares this perspective:

> *Truly I tell you, whoever does not receive the kingdom of God as a little child will never enter it.*
> **Mark 10:15**

The Gospel of Luke shares admonitions about children and the kingdom of God that are almost identical [Luke 18:15–17]. Jesus does not mean that only those who received the Christian message while they were children will receive salvation, but he

76

does mean that we must be child-like in our relationships with God if we are to receive what God wishes to give us.

As congregations, we need to welcome children in the same spirit that Jesus did. We need to welcome the children for their own sake, for the sake of their parents, and for the sake of what we learn from children.

Many congregations are not comfortable with the presence of children. Have you been in churches which:

• had several adults who complained if children made noise during the worship service?

• were reluctant to provide child care to make it easier for young parents to attend classes and other groups?

• gave relatively low priority to the recruitment of teachers and other children's leaders, conveying the view that those positions were not as important as property and finance positions in the church?

• had children's sermons in which the speaker really addressed the adults more than the children, sometimes in words the children could not understand?

• had difficulty recruiting people to work with children's classes, choirs, and small groups?

Some of those questions may be descriptive of what has happened in your congregation. If our enthusiasm for the presence of children isn't high and they aren't given a priority in our programming, we need to reevaluate what we consider to be important in the church.

What Do We Offer Children?

A study of "Children and the Church" shows that many congregations have work to do in being as supporting and welcoming of children as they should be. Most of us need to

77

spend more time looking at the church through the eyes of children like Jessica and also through the eyes of parents of young children. That study showed that far too many of our congregations have simply not evaluated their programs, practices, and attitudes regarding children.

The chart on the next page comes from the "Children and the Church" study and shows the attitudes toward children reflected in various program offerings and strategies in over three hundred congregations.

Note that the vast majority of churches do provide child care on Sunday. Virtually all of the churches not doing so were very small congregations and generally had only one or two small children who were present. Only about one in five congregations, however, had child care available on a regular basis for persons attending midweek programs, classes, and meetings. Many said it was not provided because it was not needed. Unfortunately, it isn't easy to measure the accuracy of such statements. The failure to make child care available can be a self-fulfilling prophecy, with people simply not coming when it is not available. While many congregations do have a mature adult staffing the nursery or other child care, almost as many rely primarily on teenagers for that function. Repeated studies, however, show that parents who are visiting like the security of leaving infants and young children with mature adults.

Slightly more than two-thirds of those participating in the study had a children's sermon as a regular part of Sunday morning worship. Many of those, however, acknowledged that much of the content of the children's sermon was aimed at adults. Obviously adults can gain from what is said to children, but we don't want children to perceive that part of the worship service in the way Jessica did. The children's sermon, if a part of the service, should be directed at the children, keeping their needs and language abilities in mind. Adults will still gain from its presence!

About forty percent of the churches in the study offered junior church for at least part of the year. Junior church or children's church programs take children into a worship environment of their own for all of the worship service or for a part of the worship service. The most common arrangement was for children to stay in the sanctuary with their parents through the children's sermon and then to go to a separate area for the remainder of the service—thus sparing them the pastor's sermon and sparing their parents the challenge of keeping them occupied constructively in the pews.

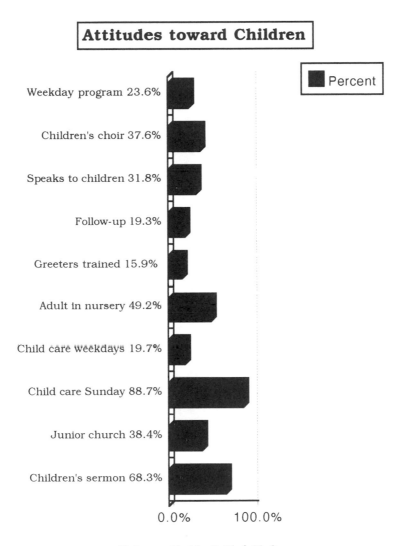

Attitudes toward Children

Data provided by Faith & Media

Some of those who participated in the study were philosophically opposed to junior church, feeling that children gained the most from remaining in the sanctuary through the whole service. Those churches often provided coloring books and crayons or other activity materials for children. (Some churches which had junior church also made activity materials available for the portion of time children were in the sanctuary with their parents.) Slightly more than one out of four churches which did not offer junior church indicated that they wished to do so but had difficulty finding adequate volunteers for that purpose.

Almost forty percent of the churches had a children's choir of some kind. Medium-sized and larger congregations often had two or more children's choirs. These choirs normally did not perform on a weekly basis but were a part of worship once or twice a month. In interviews which were part of the research project, those who had a children's choir indicated that worship attendance was generally higher on the Sundays the choir performed.

About one in four churches had some kind of program through the week (other than day care or nursery school) which could be used for outreach to children who were not already part of the life of the church. Some saw the children's choir functioning in that kind of way because of the time rehearsals were scheduled during the week, but several congregations offered a midweek recreation program, tutoring program, Christian education program, or other activity aimed at reaching children both inside and outside of the church family. These churches were the ones most likely to report growing attendance of children and parents on Sunday morning.

Fewer than one in five churches provided any training to greeters or ushers in how to respond to children. Thus children are often ignored or treated to the kind of head-patting which Jessica resented.

Likewise, fewer than one in five churches had any systematic plan for following up with children who visited. There was very often follow-up on the parents, but children were generally assumed to be covered by that same process. A minority of the churches participating in the study did have a teacher, another children's worker, a child, or the parent of a child make a phone call or another form of outreach to any child who visited worship or Sunday school. Those churches which did so were very satisfied with the results and felt it had helped children who came as visitors feel more accepted and more interested in continuing to come.

Large numbers of congregations have some kind of day care or nursery school as part of the church's program or have a separately incorporated day care or nursery school which utilizes the congregation's facilities. Those which saw the day care or nursery school program as a part of the church's overall ministry were the ones most likely to report receiving new members through that entry point.

A still small but rapidly growing number of congregations have moved their major Christian education thrust to a weekday evening *instead of* Sunday morning. Those churches often do this on Wednesday or Thursday evening and include classes for all ages and a meal. Some churches offer an extensive mid-week program like this *in addition to* a traditional Sunday school. The Children and the Church study, as already shared, showed that midweek Christian education opportunities for children definitely help strengthen attendance of children and parents on Sunday morning.

To our knowledge, there have not been any large-scale, objective studies which measured the impact of those mid-week Christian education programs which replace rather than simply supplement Sunday morning Christian education. Our observation is that the most successful programs of this kind are those in new congregations which have from the beginning decided to do mid-week Christian education rather than traditional Sunday school. If a church has a strong Sunday school program in place, it is probably a better strategy to use a mid-week program as a supplement rather than as a replacement.

Strategies for Greater Hospitality to Children

Several clear strategies emerge as ways to increase the hospitality of the congregation both to the children who already are part of its life and to those who are visitors.

1. The church needs to evaluate the nursery and child care areas from the perspective of children and parents:

81

• These areas should be spotlessly clean and attractive.

• The person in charge should be a mature adult with whom parents will feel comfortable leaving children. The need for this is in no way intended to be disrespectful of the excellent child care provided by many teenagers. Teenagers can certainly be part of the child care process, but parents who do not know the particular teenagers will feel better when a mature adult is present.

• Those who staff the nursery or child care should check with parents to know their names and to inquire about any other needed information relative to the care of their children. Ask what class the parents will be visiting during the Sunday school time so that it would be easy to find them in an emergency. Some churches even give parents beeping or vibrating pager units which can be carried and which give a clear beep or a soundless vibration if the parents are needed in the nursery. This can be particularly valuable in large congregations.

2. Sunday school classes (or other Christian education settings for children) should be evaluated from the standpoint of both children and parents. For example:

• Be sure there are adequate numbers of leaders for all children's classes. The younger the children, the greater the need for a small student-teacher ratio. This helps eliminate discipline problems, spreads the responsibility of following up on absent members and visitors, and makes possible greater personalization.

• Be sure the classrooms are clean and attractive—not only to adults but more importantly to children. Be sure that tables and chairs are an appropriate size for the age of the students.

• Have leaders teach the children how to respond to guests. Like adults, children benefit from instruc-

82

tion in how to extend hospitality. Jessica had a very good experience because of the way one class member in particular related to her. Introductions need to be made, and there should be efforts to help children learn the names of one another. Name tags can be a help if a class has the good fortune to enjoy frequent guests.

Help the children in classes and groups learn how to extend hospitality to one another and to guests!

- Students should be encouraged to reach out to their own friends who don't have church homes and invite them to Sunday school and other children's activities.

- Respond to children who visit in a systematic way, either with a phone call or an offer to share in another activity during the week. Other children in the class can do this with middle and upper elementary age children. A teacher or the parent of a student needs to do it for younger classes.

- Some classes find it helpful to have fruit juice or another light snack available.

- Leaders need to know how to respond to visiting parents—be sure they are clear on whether to pick up the children or if the children are to find them in fellowship area (if the children are old enough to do so).

- Leaders need to follow up on those who break a pattern of regular attendance. Though many cute cards are available for this purpose ("We've been missing you" accompanied by a photo of a dog or cat, for example), a phone call usually is a better follow-up procedure. A card or letter will occasionally be misinterpreted as being critical of the absence.

• Leaders need to get the name, address, and phone number of the visitors, so that follow-up is easy to do. This information may also be useful to others working at outreach if the visitors failed to sign a guest registration for the worship service (assuming they attended the worship service).

• Leaders need to use a variety of teaching methods. Children need movement and change of pace if they are to remain interested in what they are studying. While it's certainly true that classes should be more than entertainment, there's no reason for them to be boring!

• Class parties are a great idea. Some classes also find it meaningful to celebrate the birthdays of students.

For more suggestions on creative teaching methods, the development of warmth in the classroom, and techniques for reaching out through Christian education, see **Reaching Out through Christian Education** by Steve Clapp and Jerry O. Cook (listed in the Resources and References chapter at the end of this book).

3. As already suggested, greeters and ushers need training in how to respond to children. Children appreciate being addressed directly in conversation rather than being talked about. Remember the feelings of Jessica! Adults who are especially tall sometimes bend or kneel to greet young children. Greeters should know where classrooms are for various age levels.

4. The worship service should also respond to the needs of children. Ways to accomplish that include:

• Having coloring books, crayons, or other activity materials available for children to use during the service.

• Having a "Children's Corner Cart" at the entrance to the sanctuary with books that children can read during the service.

- Having a children's choir in which children can participate. As mentioned earlier, these choirs usually sing in worship once or twice a month rather than every week.

- Having at least one part of the service which is especially focused on the needs and interests of children. This may be an anthem by the children's choir, a children's sermon, a puppet drama, or any other strategy which speaks especially to children.

- Those who do the part of the service especially directed at children should be taught to speak directly to the children, using appropriate words, but also cautioned not to "speak down" to the children or to use the children's time to deliver a message which is primarily for adults.

- The minister and other worship leaders should model acceptance and appreciation of children. When a baby cries, a worship leader might say: "The sound of children is the sound of a healthy church!" Those who serve as greeters and ushers should be prepared to give reassurance to parents who are obviously concerned about minor behavioral problems.

- In addition to modeling acceptance and appreciation of children, the pastor should also teach the congregation why children are important to the church and how they can be helped to feel at home. Adults should place just as much priority on learning the names of children as the names of parents.

- When remodeling an existing sanctuary or building a new sanctuary, keep children in mind! Use carpeting and fabrics that are stain resistant so that parents can feel free to give their children drinks in the sanctuary. Think about the comfort of the seating for children as well as for adults.

5. Junior church or children's church can be a blessing to both children and their parents. Such services, as already discussed, make it possible for children to share in activities that are age-appropriate rather than becoming bored with the sermon and other aspects of the worship service. Some parents can participate more meaningfully in the worship service if they are not having to worry about a fidgeting child.

Many churches choose to have children remain in the sanctuary through a children's anthem or children's sermon and then have them go to a separate location for junior church. This lets children become accustomed to the sanctuary setting and feel a part of the service without keeping them there for the entire time.

If your church is too small in membership for junior church or children's church to be realistic, don't be concerned about that. Having books to read, pictures to color, and other activities available for children can meet some of the same needs as junior church.

If you do have junior church, be sure that the activities for children are ones they will enjoy and from which they can learn. One of the authors of this book has attended some junior church services at which the children were expected to sit quietly in chairs while an adult read biblical passages to them and gave them a mini-sermon. That strategy gains little over having the children stay in the sanctuary. Junior church certainly may include some Bible study and some stories, but the setting should be relaxed and there should be craft activities and other opportunities for movement.

6. The needs of children should be taken into consideration during any kind of fellowship time. In addition to coffee and tea for adults, be sure to have cocoa or fruit drink for children. Some adults will also prefer the cocoa or fruit drink. If your church uses "silent greeters" during the fellowship time to be sure that no one is ignored, instruct those persons to be alert for the needs of children as well.

Church leaders also need to model tolerance of the behavior of children during fellowship times. If children have been very quiet during worship services, they may have pent-up energy. If the fellowship area has adequate space, adults should not be

86

upset because children choose to play games during the fellowship time.

7. Familiar faces are important to children! When class leadership is changed too quickly, new children may become disoriented and confused. Younger children especially need continuity. While many of us as adults like systems of rotating teachers and child care providers, those systems are not always the best for children who tend to like the familiarity of people they've seen before. It's also great to be present one week as a guest and to be called by name when one returns the next week.

8. Being known by one's own name is important. No one likes to be known simply as "Fred's daughter" or "Mary's son" or "the youngest Stafford boy." Adults need to be encouraged to learn the names of children!

9. Discipline problems, when they arise, need to be handled with tact and consideration. How would you want to be treated if you were a child again? How would parents want their children treated? Obviously there are not always easy answers to discipline problems, but some strategies can help:

- Having a sufficient number of adult leaders often makes a great difference. A class of fifth graders that averaged twelve out-of-control children each week became a fun, reasonably controlled fifteen when two adults leaders were added to the single teacher who had been working with the class before.

- Talking with children alone about discipline problems, if possible, is almost always preferable to doing so in front of the class.

- Appealing to children who are troublemakers to help create a better atmosphere in the class can be an effective strategy—that makes them part of the solution to the problem!

- Talking with the parents can sometimes help a class leader better understand the reasons for the behavior of children. Sometimes having the parent of a difficult child come share in class sessions for a couple of weeks can make a difference.

10. With children, as with adults, it's important for a quick response to be made when there is a break in what has been a pattern of regular attendance. That was mentioned in relationship to Sunday school classes but it's also important in terms of children's choirs, junior church, worship attendance, and any other children's activities.

11. When a church has a day care or nursery school program through the week, opportunities should be sought for the church to show hospitality to those children and their parents. This can be an excellent port of entry to the church for those with no church home. Consider:

- Having the pastor share in greeting children and their parents on at least an occasional basis.

- Having a place for information on church membership as a part of the registration process so that you can be aware of persons who do not have a church home.

- Offering occasional parties or fellowship times with refreshments for children and parents. These can be an ideal opportunities for the pastor and other church leaders to visit with parents and children.

- Offering seminars on topics such as "Developing the Spiritual Life of Children" or "Creating a Secure Family Environment" to the parents of children. Have those taught by the pastor or by another church leader.

- Have low-key phone calls made, inviting parents to come with their children to worship services or to special events at the church.

- Consider having a different tuition or fee scale for persons who belong to the congregation! This rewards those who already do attend and can be a motivation for others to try out your church.

12. Be sensitive to children with special needs. Orientation for teachers should include alerting them to the fact that some children may have difficulty reading and should not be put on the spot in front of others. If students have physical, mental, or emotional limitations, some special arrangements may be appropriate. Special needs can sometimes be opportunities for innovative programs. Some congregations, for example, have begun midweek programs for children with Attention Deficit Disorder (called, for example, ADDventure).

13. Be alert for additional program opportunities that can help meet the needs of children. Is there a need for a midweek recreation program? A tutoring program? A Bible study group? A drama group for upper elementary children? Midweek groups can sometimes be an especially excellent opportunity for children to bring their friends who are not part of any local church.

Some churches have started Girls' Clubs which are midweek opportunities for girls only. Activities include baking cookies to take to nursing homes, learning how to handle money, learning about career opportunities, painting a room in the church or a room in the home of an elderly person, going to movies together, developing a recycling program for the church, and more! A Girls' Club can meet anywhere from once a week to once a month and can be an excellent port of entry for new people into the congregation.

14. Be sure that your promotional materials and strategies make it clear that children are valued in your congregation! That should be a part of your church brochure, of any newspaper advertisements, of your church website, and of any special canvassing materials. Include pictures of children in your promotional materials.

15. Involve children who are already in your church in helping you evaluate your programs. Get their input! What would make worship and classes better? What opportunities would they like? What help do they need in extending hospitality to others?

16. Provide opportunities for children to interact with older members of the congregation. Most older persons are in fact eager for positive contact with children. Those persons who seem to be crabby toward children are often that way because they have not had sufficient opportunity to interact with children in recent years. Do things like:

• Having children give flowers out to older members on a special occasion.

• Having a "secret friends" system between a children's class and an adult class.

• Having a children's class host an adult class at a dinner.

• Having a children's class survey an adult class on a particular issue.

• Having an adult class survey a children's class on a particular issue.

Welcoming Teenagers

Concept: Teenagers are struggling for identity and coping with a multitude of pressures. The church's hospitality should offer them a safe place to be themselves and to grow in their relationships with Christ and other people.

Jennifer just celebrated her sixteenth birthday but looks and in many respects acts as though she's twenty. She enjoys the senior high youth group of a suburban Protestant church but considers herself considerably more mature than the other group members. Her relationship with Rick, who is a sophomore in college, and her part-time job as a clerk in a department store are both greater priorities to her than involvement with the church. She is concerned about her relationship with Christ but also feels that some of the church's teachings are too narrow for today. She has many homosexual friends, doesn't feel abortion is necessarily wrong, and has been having an active sexual relationship with Rick for more than a year. Jennifer's parents divorced when she was fourteen, and her mother has remarried. She spends most of her time at the home of her mother and stepfather but occasionally visits her father on weekends.

The same youth group has Diane, who is fifteen years old but, much to her regret, looks like eleven. She's very bright and also deeply committed to the church. Her views, unlike Jennifer's, are relatively conservative. She doesn't approve of homosexuality or abortion and says that people shouldn't make love unless they are married. The church holds top priority for her, and she's the kind of teenager most teachers and youth group leaders love to have—except for the occasions when her intensity and refusal to compromise make her a little hard to take!

Diane's mother and father divorced when she was nine, and her father has remarried. Her father and stepmother live in another state, and Diane and her younger sister live with their mother, who has chosen not to remarry.

Joel is seventeen, and his appearance makes most adults crazy. He wears his hair long, has tattoos on both arms and his back, and wears metal in his ears, his nose, and his tongue. His preferred music is heavy metal, and his preferred drink is Coors. He's fairly loyal to the youth group, but adult leaders can count on his taking the minority or unpopular position on any issue. Employment would probably keep him away from the youth group except that he seems unable to hold any job for more than a few days. At times it seems like he simply enjoys arguing, but he also displays considerable gentleness to people who are having problems. He really admires the pastor and will do almost anything the pastor requests. That same respect, however, doesn't extend to the youth group advisors. Most people do not know that Joel attempted suicide when he was fifteen.

Matt, who is fourteen, admires Joel and has a large collection of CDs, purchased primarily on Joel's recommendations. Matt, however, is not comfortable with controversy and tries hard to get along with adults. Since he's more clean-cut in appearance, people in the church keep suggesting that he try to influence Joel's appearance. That, of course, isn't going to happen, since Matt would look like Joel if he weren't so concerned about the approval of his parents and other adults. He seems to embrace the Christian faith and gladly helps with service projects, but his Sunday school teacher and his youth group advisor both wonder how deeply rooted his faith really is.

Angie, sixteen, has just moved to town and has started attending the youth group which includes Jennifer, Diane, Joel, Matt, and seven other teenagers. Angie lived in a rural community until this move and was very active in a small church that was surrounded by cornfields. She feels more than a little overwhelmed by her new environment but is trying to act as though she finds everything exciting rather than scary. She likes the kids in the suburban youth group but is still trying to figure out whether or not Joel means some of the far-out things he says. She especially likes Jennifer but feels as though Jennifer is already too involved with other people to make much time for a new friendship. The church has always been very important to Angie, and she's looking forward to the summer work trip that's being planned.

Cassie at fifteen years of age has a family situation that differs from the others in the group. Three years earlier her mother came out as a lesbian, divorced Cassie's father, and started living with another woman. Cassie was an only child and stayed primarily with her father for the two years following the divorce. Now that has changed. Her father married a woman with three children, all of them boys and one the same age as Cassie. Her father's home had been a refuge for her while she sorted out how she felt about her mother and her mother's "friend." Now she had to deal with another new family, and she wasn't sure how she felt about it. One impact of her father's remarriage, however, had been for her to start spending more time at her mother's house.

She was slowly beginning to accept her mother's sexual orientation and had begun to genuinely like her mother's partner. In time she expects that she will like her father's new wife and the three stepbrothers, but it all feels a little overwhelming. During the "joys and concerns" sharing time of the youth group, Cassie usually has something to say. She appreciates the way the members of the group listen to her and pray for her and affirm her. She resents Diane's judgmental views toward homosexual people, but Diane has been less vocal since the time that her words brought Cassie to tears. Diane never intended to hurt her so deeply. Cassie had stayed away from the group for a month but returned when Diane called her to apologize for not being more sensitive.

Understanding Teenagers Today

Although the names have been changed, all six of the young people just described are members of the same youth group. They reflect the kind of diversity that adult leaders are finding in youth groups around North America. These are teens who aren't going to agree on everything, but they are also capable of extending significant support to each other.

There has probably never been an easy day to be a teenager, and our present day is no exception. Adults who work with youth are continually challenged to understand the complex and rapidly changing culture in which teens are growing up. Consider these aspects of life for today's young people:

1. **More young people than ever spend at least part of their childhood in a single parent home**, and many others divide their time between two households: one with a mother and stepfather and one with a father and stepmother. Some, like Cassie, may have a parent who is in a homosexual relationship. Children of different marriages also get mixed in the households.

2. **Teenagers continue to be heavily influenced by the media**, with many spending around twenty-five hours a week watching television. Computers and the Internet have also had powerful influence on today's teens. The Internet brings access to all sorts of information and also makes possible the development of relationships with persons in other parts of the country or the world. Teens are also comfortable with computers and the Internet in a way that many adults are not.

3. **Music pervades the culture of teenagers** with heavy metal, rock, rap, country-western, and alternative all having considerable influence. Contemporary Christian music connects with some teenagers but not as strongly as some of their parents would like. While the music of one generation has not always sat well with other generations, parents today do seem to have more openness to and appreciation of the music of their teenage children than some past generations have had. It continues to be difficult to truly understand teens without understanding at least some of their music.

4. **Teens are being raised in an extremely materialistic, money-conscious culture.** Adult society has done an excellent job teaching youth some very questionable values: that people who earn more money are better people than those who are poor; that the primary standard for evaluating success is financial; that the purpose of getting an education is to get a job to earn more money; and that one's own financial needs come before the needs of others.

Many young people are hearing all those messages about affluence but are themselves growing up in poverty. Black youth are at least four times more likely than white youth to be in families with incomes below the poverty level, and Native

American youth are twice again as likely to be in poverty situations. Poor youth, however, are very often not involved in churches.

Youth of all economic backgrounds are more likely than ever to have part-time employment during the school year and full-time employment during the summer months. Many fast-food restaurants are heavily dependent on the teenage employees whom they pay minimum wage or only a little more. The major use of money from part-time and summer employment is in the provision of an automobile.

5. Appearance is of enormous importance to teenagers. The Jewish and Christian faiths teach that we are created in the image of God, and the Old and New Testaments speak of the value of the body. We live in a culture which promotes certain body images through advertising, television shows, motion pictures, and the Internet. Thin women and well-muscled men are the norm in the entertainment industry, and most ordinary people don't meet those standards of attractiveness.

Steve Clapp and his Christian Community colleagues conducted a study of almost six thousand teenagers to explore the relationship between their faith and their sexual values and decisions. The teens who participated in the study were all active members of congregations. The teens in this study were asked to choose from one of four options to describe how happy they were with their bodies. The chart on the next page shows the responses from the young people, and you can see significant differences between the way that teenage males and teenage females feel about their bodies. Among the females in this study, 61.9% were somewhat or definitely unhappy with their bodies; 19.5% were happy but still wanted some improvement; and only 18.6% were happy without qualification. The comparable figures for males were 48.5% somewhat or definitely unhappy; 17.2% happy but wanting some improvement, and 24.3% happy without qualification. Almost twice as many girls as boys were "definitely unhappy" with their bodies. Still, many boys are unhappy and want changes.

(The results of that study, which will be referred to in other portions of this chapter, are published in the book *Faith Matters: Teenagers, Religion, and Sexuality*.)

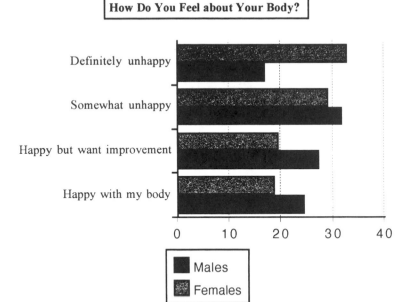

How Do You Feel about Your Body?

- Definitely unhappy
- Somewhat unhappy
- Happy but want improvement
- Happy with my body

0   10   20   30   40

■ Males
▒ Females

Data from the ***Faith Matters*** *study*

6. Large numbers of teens are sexually active. The ***Faith Matters*** study showed that, among 11th and 12th grade males who are involved in their congregations, 30.9% have had sexual intercourse, and 28.9% have had oral sex. For 11th and 12th grade females, the comparable figures are 29.0% and 26.4%. While the *Faith Matters* study reflected a lower rate of sexual intercourse for church active teens than has been found in studies of secular teens, the rates are still much higher than most clergy and parents have thought. Over 70% of 11th and 12th grade church-involved males and females have fondled a partner's breasts or genitals, and about 50% have been nude with a member of the opposite sex.

Most of these church active teenagers acknowledge that they do not have all the information they need to make sexual decisions, and the majority indicate that their congregations have done almost nothing to help them link their sexual decisions to their spiritual lives. Fewer than 14% of the youth responding indicated that they had received any significant

96

information from their faith-based institutions on decision-making about intercourse, preventing sexually transmitted diseases, preventing AIDS, rape, or homosexuality. Half of the teenagers in the *Faith Matters* study who became pregnant chose to end the pregnancy with an abortion.

7. Many churches have participating teenagers who feel that they have a homosexual or bisexual orientation. Slightly more than one out of ten males and females in the *Faith Matters* study indicated having a homosexual orientation, having a bisexual orientation, or being uncertain what their sexual orientation was.

Eighty-eight percent of the teens who self-identified as homosexual said that their pastor was not aware of their orientation. Only 36% indicated that there was a youth worker, advisor, or other adult leaders (besides a parent) in the church who was aware of their orientation. While 83% said that there was at least one young person in the church who was aware of their orientation, only 16% said that the whole youth group or class knew about the orientation. Almost half of these youth (46%) said that their parents did not know about their orientation.

Thus many of our churches have teenagers who feel that they have a homosexual or bisexual orientation but are living secret lives as far as most of the church is concerned—and half the time their own parents are not aware of their orientation. What kind of hospitality are these teens feeling in our churches? How should congregations respond to teens who are struggling with questions of sexual orientation? Most of our congregations have not adequately considered such questions.

8. Teenagers today, as in every generation, are heavily influenced by their peers. In many respects they care more about the approval of people their own age than of their parents and other adults. Some teens demonstrate significant caring for one another, but others feel isolated. Involvement in a strong church youth group can have a more positive influence on young people during these important formative years.

9. Teens today are more likely to be the victims of crime and the agents of crime alike. Some estimates place the percentage of teens who have committed theft at 10% and the percentage who have been involved in significant fighting at 28%. Most communities are locking up larger and larger numbers of teenagers, often without doing anything to lower the crime rate. Incarceration generally hardens teens and puts them under the influence of more experienced criminals.

With our increasing awareness of the potential for violence in schools, metal detectors and security officers have become part of the academic landscape. Many schools have adopted policies of "zero tolerance" for any kind of bullying or fighting behavior with violators immediately expelled. Such "get tough" policies seem on the surface to be appropriate for our time, but what happens to the youth who are expelled? Is the teen who shoves another teen in the hallway really in the same category as the teen who plots to shoot someone? Parents, teens, teachers, and school administrators are all struggling with such difficult questions. These policies and the fears that drive them have a significant impact on how young people feel about themselves, about one another, and about the school environment.

10. Teens are often the victims of physical or sexual abuse. The percentage who are abused increases steadily with age. Secular studies show that, among sixth grade males, around 14% have been physically or sexually abused; the percentage for sixth grade females is 18%. By the eleventh grade, the percentage for males has gone up to 17% and for girls all the way to 35%. Abuse also makes it about twice as likely that teens will suffer depression, lose self-esteem, and feel that they are under continuous stress. Being active in a congregation is no automatic protection against abuse. In the *Faith Matters* study, 31% of 11th and 12th grade females reported having had unwanted sexual experiences.

11. Widespread availability of alcohol and other drugs continues to be the case across North America. Percentages reported differ from study to study, but all show that abuse of alcohol stands as a far greater problem than the abuse of any illegal drugs. According to the Centers for Disease Control, as many as 31% of teenagers drink to excess, and at least 11% experiment with drugs. In certain communities, those percentages may run much higher. The use of alcohol or illegal drugs also makes it more likely that teens will have sexual intercourse and will do so without protection against pregnancy or disease. In spite of massive advertising about the dangers of tobacco, many teens continue to smoke.

12. Teens today are also more likely than ever to have problems with depression and, like Joel, to have attempted suicide. At least 15% have experienced serious depression, and estimates of those attempting suicide range from 5% to 13%. Teens who have a self-identified homosexual orientation are more likely than other teens to have considered or attempted suicide, according to the *Faith Matters* study.

13. But there's another side to teenagers today that is too often overlooked and under-publicized! For example:

• Teens are interested in spiritual matters. Gallup polls and other studies show that teens continue to be interested in spiritual life retreats.

• Teens like to do things for others. Service projects are very attractive to teens, and participation in them correlates strongly with lower levels of early sexual activity and lower levels of criminal activity.

• Teens care about their parents and continue to do so following divorces. While teens are almost unanimous in not liking divorce, they don't stop loving their parents because of it.

• While all teens seek improvement, most are relatively happy with their lives. They are happier with their lives on the whole than they are with their physical appearance!

• The kind of youth who tend to be active in our congregations are not as frequently in "at risk" categories as other teens.

14. Teens are not just the "church of tomorrow," they are the church today. Many congregations focus on youth work from the perspective of preparing young people for the future, and certainly that is important. Youth, however, are part of the church right now. They want to be involved, and they want to be taken seriously. They are often "natural evangelists" and may well reach out to their friends with invitations to church involvement more readily than adults in the church reach out to their friends. Youth can make significant contributions to worship, service projects, and church decision-making. Youth who serve on boards, commissions, committees, task forces, and mission groups of the church often bring new energy and new ideas.

What It Means To Welcome Youth

What does it mean for the church to provide a welcoming place for young people like Jennifer, Diane, Joel, Matt, Angie, and Cassie? Churches that help young people feel at home tend to be characterized by several things:

- **Welcoming congregations appreciate the fact that youth are not just the "church of tomorrow" but are in fact part of the church today.** They recognize the desire of young people to make a difference in the lives of others and provide them with opportunities to do so, not only with summer mission trips but also with late afternoon, evening, or weekend service projects. They also encourage young people to be active on boards and committees of the church, often inviting them to serve in pairs for mutual support.

- **Welcoming congregations recognize that it is crucial to provide an accepting atmosphere for teens**, regardless of superficial matters such as hairstyle and clothing. Adults who work with teens need to be helped to recognize that clothes and hair are not appropriate issues for argument in the Christian community. As uncomfortable as tattoos and tongue studs may make some adults, those should never be bases for making teens feel unwelcome.

- **Welcoming congregations take very seriously the need to provide a "safe place" for youth.** They insist that adults who work with teens and the teens themselves honor confidentiality and respect differences. Although some good-natured kidding may take place, it's important that neither Diane nor Joel, for example, be criticized or made the victim of brutal jokes because of their differences from others in the group. Both Diane's quick agreement with adult opinions and readiness to help and Joel's reluctance to share agreement or help can subject them to criticism.

The need for confidentiality is crucial. What Jennifer says about sexual activity or what Joel confesses about drinking should not be spread outside the group. There may be instances when a youth leader is sufficiently concerned about the danger of suicide to feel that something must be shared with a parent, but such instances should and must be very rare—or people will not share what they really think and feel with the group.

Youth group leaders and teachers need to recognize that they may well have teens with a self-identified homosexual or bisexual orientation. Churches differ in how they view homosexuality, but whatever the doctrines of the church, it is crucial that individual teens feel accepted and feel that they are in a "safe place" in which they can explore what the Christian faith means for their lives.

- **Welcoming congregations offer a balance of opportunities for youth** but also recognize that some teens will be more comfortable with one or two kinds of activities than with others. Give youth permission to "pick and choose."

  — Youth should have the opportunity to share in **worship** and to give leadership to congregational services. Youth choirs and other music groups can also be valuable opportunities.

  — Youth also need **learning** opportunities. They need to learn about the Bible and about how to apply those ancient teachings to contemporary life.

101

— **Recreation and social** opportunities are also quite important. Some church youth programs are criticized for being "nothing but fun," but such activities are a major part of building group identity and also provide valuable ports of entry for new young people. Encourage group members to bring guests on movie nights, on weekend retreats, to ski trips, and on summer trips.

— **Service** opportunities are also important. Those can take many forms including improvements to the church, help to senior citizens with home and yard work, the rehabilitation of neglected properties, working with a food pantry, and summer work trips to mission sites.

• **Welcoming congregations teach youth about hospitality**—how to show it to one another, to new youth like Angie, and to adults.

• **Welcoming congregations appreciate the role food can play for youth** just as it does for adults. Refreshments at youth group meetings, good food for overnight lock-ins and retreats, pizza parties to welcome new members, and meals shared between adult leaders and youth can all be part of a welcoming group atmosphere.

• **Welcoming congregations have had considerable success with mentoring programs** in which adults are paired with youth. The adult and the teenager meet together at least once a month to talk about things of concern to both of them and particularly to work on questions of values and beliefs.

• **Welcoming congregations have learned the crucial role small group sharing should play in youth work.** Larger groups need to have enough adult leaders to make it possible for some discussions to happen in small groups. Youth groups tend to level off at an average attendance of 25 no matter how great the potential number may be.

Welcoming Young Adults

> **Concept:** Almost all churches want to reach more young adults, especially young adult families. Making young adults part of the church, however, either requires change or causes change—sometimes both.

"That drama that was done at worship last week would have been just fine for some kind of evening program," said Helen Adams, who was fifty-three years old and president of the Kum Dubble class at Cedar Creek Community Church. Although not herself a member of the church board, she was speaking at their meeting by request of the class. "What we don't understand is why it was part of the worship service and replaced the sermon. Along with that, we're very concerned about the songs that we've been singing from that new loose-leaf hymnal. They simply do not sound worshipful."

"Helen, those are part of the changes that the worship committee talked to the congregation about at the annual meeting," responded Bill Avery, who was chairperson of that committee. "We've been careful to just do one song a week from the loose-leaf hymnal, and we've intentionally only done the drama once a month. Everyone seemed to like the drama last month, and no one complained about it replacing the sermon. Was there something different about this one?"

"Speaking only for myself and not for the class, this one was not as uplifting. The first drama that was done emphasized the place of forgiveness in our lives, and there was something to get out of that even without a sermon. This one seemed almost entirely about AIDS, and to tell you the truth, all it did was make us feel bad. At least that's all it did for me. There are people who come to worship who are going through very difficult times in their own lives. Mrs. Bartholomew lost her husband just two weeks ago, and Walt Adams was just released from the hospital. What was there in the drama for them? A sermon, on the other hand, usually has at least something which you can grab hold of to get you through the week, to recharge you in a sense. This one didn't do that."

"I agree that this drama was a little heavier than the first one," said Sam Walters, the pastor. "What the drama was trying to show, however, is the way that God's strength and help come to people in the midst of difficult times. The central figure in the drama did have AIDS, but I didn't see the drama being primarily about AIDS. I don't apologize for the fact that AIDS was part of it, because that's a part of contemporary life that we need to face. I saw the emphasis of the drama, however, being on the courage of the man who had the terminal illness and on the support he received from his faith and from the friendship of others. I would think that might have been helpful to Mrs. Bartholomew and to Walt Adams."

"As a matter of fact," Bill Avery offered, "I heard Walt Adams say that he appreciated the drama."

"Well, I certainly didn't mean to be speaking for him," Helen responded, "but I know that Mrs. Bartholomew was quite upset. She told me that she was."

"Then I'll certainly make a point to call on her this week," said Sam, "and I do appreciate your calling that to my attention."

"Pastor Sam," Helen continued, "I am truly grateful for all the hard work you've done for our congregation, and I think the others in the Kum Dubble class agree with me. But when we were talking about some changes coming to worship, you said that one of the major reasons was to try and reach young adults. We've been using the new hymnal for two months now, and we've had two dramas instead of sermons. Where are the new young adults? I don't see them coming!"

"Have you invited any to come yourself?" asked Barb Wolinski, who chaired the membership commission. "Remember, that was part of the plan. All of us have been encouraged to invite the people we know, especially young adults."

"No, I haven't," answered Helen. "I don't know that many

104

young adults; quite frankly, I don't feel good enough about what is happening in our services to invite anyone I do know. Barb, you're one of the few young adults active in our congregation. We're dependent on people like you to invite others your age."

"My husband and I have invited another couple, as a matter of fact," said Barb. "They came to the first service that had a drama in it, and they returned two more times. They've been gone or had company the last couple of weekends so they weren't here for this drama."

"You mean the nice young couple who had a little girl with them and sat right between you and your husband?" Helen asked.

"Yes," answered Barb.

"Well, I hadn't realized those were prospective members. The way you and your husband with interacting with them and the way your husband kept their daughter on his lap through the service, I just assumed that they were relatives of yours. But those must have been the only ones so far."

"Yes," agreed Sam. "Those probably are the only ones so far. We all need to be inviting more people. I think it is true that some of us don't know a lot of young adults who aren't already involved in a church somewhere else in town. But I think a greater problem is that we often don't feel comfortable talking about our faith and the church. We're planning to have some small groups during Lent to help us all become more comfortable reaching out to others."

"Then there doesn't seem to be a lot of point in continuing to do different things in worship if it will be Lent before we have the training for the next step in outreach," argued Helen.

"Some of us," Barb said, striving hard to keep the irritation out of her voice, "are going to be inviting more people. What we are doing is creating a more contemporary environment for the people we do get to visit. Drama speaks much more effectively to some people my age than a sermon. No offense to you, Sam, but that just isn't my favorite medium. I'm glad the sermon does help others, and I wouldn't want drama every week if that was going to be hard on Mrs. Bartholomew or Helen or anyone else.

We need some drama, though, to help younger people feel it's worthwhile to connect with us here. And then the songs, Helen. I don't want to be offensive, but some of the hymns that mean a lot to you don't speak to me at all. What about 'Are Ye Able?' That one gets me every time. We sing back 'Yes, we are able,' when we know that we're not. The traditional hymns that we sing and the music that the organist plays are actually not the favorite kind of music for most of the population. Only about 4% of the public prefer classical and organ music."

Helen sighed. "This is more complicated than I'd thought. Now I see why Sam tried to get us to consider starting a second service so that one could be traditional and the other contemporary. It's hard to mix the two. I know that we need new members; I just wish there was another way to do it."

Young Adult Perspectives

Virtually all congregations want more members, and most have a special desire to reach those in the young adult years (18–35). Many older members, however, end up feeling like Helen: they want to reach new members but aren't especially enthused about the changes that are part of that process.

And change is part of the process of growth, especially when the church seeks young adults. Most churches have to go through change in order to attract and involve young adults; but even if more young adults are reached without significant change, their presence in the life of the church will itself cause change!

The meeting described at the beginning of this chapter took place in a congregation in the southeastern part of the United States, but similar conversations have occurred in many other places. Sharing that example is not meant to convey that more contemporary worship services are always necessary to reach young adults, but changes in worship are certainly a significant part of what is happening in many congregations around North America. It's also important to note that there are some twenty-two-year-olds who prefer traditional music and some fifty-three-year-olds who prefer contemporary sounds. The generalizations, however, do tend to hold in most congregations.

Consider some of the ways in which the perspective of young adults may differ from that of older adults in the church:

1. Young adults are more likely to appreciate more contemporary worship services. Young adults are not as likely as older adults to appreciate the traditional hymns, classical anthems, and organ music of most local churches. This is especially true for those young adults who did not grow up involved in a local congregation.

Although truly great preaching tends to influence most people, ministers can have an especially difficult time making the connection with young adults. (There's also a shortage of truly great preaching, but that's a topic for another book!) Young adults have, for the most part, been raised in a television and computer-oriented society in which the attention spans required on any given topic are relatively short. A sermon can require as much as thirty or forty minutes of undivided attention. The sermon as a medium simply does not hold attention as well as a medium like drama or video. Increasing numbers of churches are using drama or video instead of the sermon or are using drama or video to enhance the message of the sermon.

In our book **Worship and Hospitality**, we urge both older and younger persons in the church to think about worship in terms of hospitality. When we look at worship through the lens of hospitality, our focus shifts away from what we personally want and moves to concern for what others experience through the service of worship. Looking at worship through the lens of hospitality, we become concerned:

- About what those who are older than we are experience in the service of worship.

- About what those who are younger than we are experience in the service of worship.

- About what guests to the congregation experience in the service of worship.

- About what appeal the service of worship could have to unchurched persons if we are able to get them to share with us.

107

We recognize the presence of Christ in all of those persons, and we want to respond with love and warmth to our Lord. Viewing worship through the lens of hospitality doesn't mean that we abandon our own preferences for the style of worship we experience, but it does mean that we make our own preferences secondary to the needs of others rather than the primary criterion for how we feel about the service.

2. Young adults tend to be more informal about church. As discussed in the chapter *Welcoming Strangers*, casual clothing has become more common at work and in the church, especially among young adults. Some congregations intentionally ask ushers to dress in a variety of ways as a visual message to visitors that they should feel free to dress however they wish. Pictures that are part of church brochures and websites should show people in casual dress rather than just in suits and ties.

3. Troubles with the justice system are part of life for some young adults. The problem, in fact, is perhaps not as much that young adults today are committing more criminal acts than in the past, but rather that law enforcement authorities are so much more vigorous in their prosecution of offenders. A young adult today arrested for a crime is **three or four times** more likely to be incarcerated for it than his or her boomer counterpart twenty years ago. A person of any age today is also more likely to be locked up for a nonviolent crime than was the case twenty years ago. Currently more than one out of four young adult black men is in prison, on probation, or on parole. That's more than are enrolled in college. The United States locks up more people per hundred thousand population than any other country in the world, including South Africa. [Information shared here comes from the U.S. Department of Justice.]

When we talk with young adults about church membership, we are more likely than in the past to encounter some who have had very unpleasant experiences with law enforcement. That doesn't mean they won't respond positively to the church—the question is how the church will respond to them. Remember that in the hospitality practiced in the Ancient Near East, the burden was always on the host rather than on the guest.

4. Financial prospects for young adults today may not be as positive as in some past generations. While many new jobs have been created in recent years, a depressing number of them are in minimum wage and part-time positions. College graduates still do much better than others, but the opportunities are not as good in many fields. The cost of a college education has also skyrocketed at the same time that grants and scholarships have become harder to obtain. Increasing numbers of college and trade school students must rely on borrowing money to complete college, and that debt hangs over them for years.

The percentage of young adults owning homes has decreased since the early seventies, as shown in the following chart:

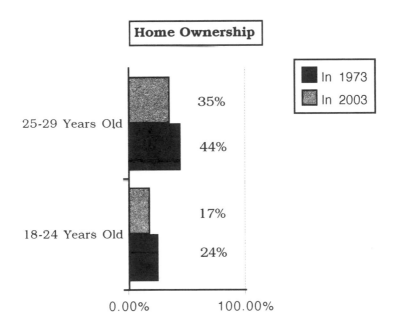

Data from the American Demographic Association

For a variety of economic reasons, rental housing has also become more expensive in some parts of the country. [In part, tax laws in the early eighties lowered some of the incentives for investing in rental housing by making rental unit owners depreciate their properties in different ways. This has caused them to make fewer investments in rental housing and to want to recover more money as they rent the housing they already own.]   One of the results of this situation is that a larger percentage of young adults in the 18–24 year-old range are living with their parents or other relatives than in the past.   Lower interest rates have helped some young adults purchase their own homes, but the lower interest rates are not enough to fully offset the shortage of high-paying jobs and debts from college. Finances have understandably become a greater priority for young adults.   The following chart shows how goals of college freshmen have changed.

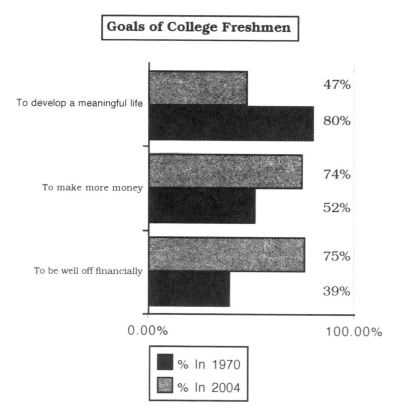

Goals of College Freshmen

To develop a meaningful life — 47% / 80%

To make more money — 74% / 52%

To be well off financially — 75% / 39%

0.00%   100.00%

■ % In 1970
▨ % In 2004

Data from the American Demographic Association
(Horizontal numbers indicate percentage feeling each is a major goal.)

5. The nature of "family" has changed for all ages, and this is particularly evident with young adults.   There was a time when talking about a "young family" brought an image of a husband, a wife, two children, a dog, and a cat living together in a ranch-style home. That isn't true today. The percentage of young adults who are married has gone down over the last thirty years.

People are remaining single longer than in the past, and they are not as likely to have children right after they are married. Another continuing trend that causes concern for many church commentators is that an increasing number of young singles are living with each other without being married. Many of those couples do end up marrying each other, but they may live together for two to five years before making that commitment.

Before being too judgmental about the trend of young adults living with each other before getting married, those of us who are older need to remember that high divorce rates have greatly impacted the childhood and adolescence of today's young adults. Many of them have grown up floating from a home with their father and stepmother to a home with their mother and step-father. Perhaps we should not be surprised that some young adults have become more cynical and more cautious about marriage. The average length of a first marriage in the United States in 2003 was eight years.

Young adults in general are more accepting of homosexual orientation and homosexual behavior than are older adults. As a result, it is not unusual to see persons of young adult age who are more open about a homosexual orientation or lifestyle than older adults are comfortable being. The willingness to hide sexual orientation in the church, which characterized many of the teens in the **Faith Matters** study (discussed in the last chapter), is not shared by most young adults of that orientation.

The chart on the next page shows that the percentage of unmarried mothers has continued to increase. The overall percentage of single parents has risen not only because of unmarried mothers but also because of the divorce rate. Large numbers of today's young adults spent part of their childhood in single-parent homes, and some of those same persons are themselves now single parents.

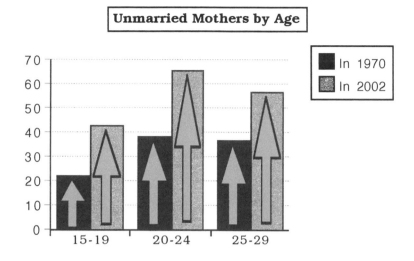

Data from the National Centers for Disease Control
Births per 1,000 unmarried women.
Unmarried women are defined as those not married at the time of the child's birth.

When we talk about reaching out as congregations to young adults, we need to be thinking not only about married couples, both with children and without children, but also about young adult singles and single parents. Our churches need to learn how to be as welcoming to an unmarried mother and her child as to a newlywed couple.

We also need to face the challenge of how we respond to young adults who live with each other but are not married and young adults who have an openly homosexual orientation or lifestyle. While denominations and congregations differ in how they feel about these life situations, the biblical admonition to show hospitality to others is not qualified to exclude those persons who may make us feel uncomfortable.

6. Young adults tend to view the church differently than older adults and are far more likely to be critical when the church seems like a bureaucracy. A study done in 2003 asked young adults who were not church members, young adults who were church members, and older adults who were church members to share their impressions of the church as a bureaucracy and of the importance of being a church member. Some striking differences emerge:

Statement	19–35 Nonm.	19–35 Memb.	36 & Older Memb.
The local church is too much like an institution or a bureaucracy.	71%	63%	39%
You can be a good Christian even though you don't belong to a local church.	86%	76%	34%

LifeQuest research results, 2003.

There are clearly differences between nineteen to thirty-five-year-olds who are not members of a church and those who are, but the most intriguing differences are between young adults who are church members and older adults who are church members. The differences are sufficiently great that it's not difficult to understand the existence of some tensions between younger adults and older adults in many congregations.

Many young adults who completed the survey commented that the decision-making structures of the local church are just too slow. Several young adults also feel that churches are too concerned with finances and need to show more concern for the spiritual life of members and for service to the community. When asked if they had shared these concerns within their local churches, the majority of those surveyed said they had not. One wrote: "I really like the older members of the church, and they've made me feel accepted. I don't want to offend them, which I would if I tried to explain why it drives me crazy to spend forty minutes in a meeting deciding whether to serve peanut butter sandwiches or cheese sandwiches to go along with the chili at an all-church supper. It took us five months to get approval to paint the room our class meets in. We volunteered to buy the paint and do the work, but it still had to go through all these approval stages by property, the trustees, and the board."

Older adult members, of course, also have their anxieties. One concerned member who was in his sixties wrote: "I know

113

that a lot of our younger members don't like to be involved in the boards and committees. It feels to them like it takes too much time to accomplish anything, and they're probably right. But the church has almost four hundred members, and we don't have the right to just do what we want because we've been elected to a position. There are procedures to be followed."

A great many young adults are also not convinced that one must be a member of a local church in order to be a Christian. This is true not only for those who aren't involved in a church but also for many who are thoroughly involved. Older members of the church tend to view the local congregation as part of the body of Christ and cannot conceive of being a Christian in isolation. No doubt this difference in perspective has a lot to do with the lower numbers of young adults who actually join a local church.

A similar survey was conducted in 1993 and in 1994. The results of the 2003 survey are very similar, with two exceptions. First, the percentage of older adults who feel the local church is too much like an institution or a bureaucracy has increased by 9% over the decade. Second, the percentage of older adults who feel you can be a good Christian even if you don't belong to a local church has increased by 13%.

Welcoming Young Adults

Obviously we can't erase the differences in life experience or in perspective between young adults and older adults. Most of the churches in North America have disproportionate numbers of older adults. If your church is one of those fortunate enough to be an exception, you are probably already doing several of the things suggested here. We especially recommend:

- **Helping older adults in the church better understand the perspective of young adults** both inside and outside of the church. Your involvement of church groups in a study of this book is one way to accomplish that. You may also want to study the coming book by Steve Clapp titled *One Hundred Ways to Reach Young Singles, Couples, and Families.* When possible, involve both young adults and older

114

adults in the study process so that you have good sharing.

• **Implement as many of the suggestions as possible from the chapter on *Welcoming Children*.** Creating an atmosphere attractive to children is one of the best possible ways to create an atmosphere that is welcoming for their parents.

• **Help members of the congregation be sure that they are just as welcoming to young singles and to couples who do not have children as they are to young couples with children.** Young adult couples who do not yet have children are usually not appreciative of the suggestion that surely they'll be starting to have them soon! Even if your church doesn't have any young adult singles, it's still possible to warmly welcome singles who visit. Older members of the congregation sometimes "adopt" young adult singles, inviting into their homes for meals and taking an interest in their lives. When you've gotten a few visitors transformed to active participants, you have the core group for a young singles group. The same can be true for married couples without children.

• **Make a special effort to help older members understand the unique circumstances of single parents.** These persons are often very interested in spiritual issues and in what the church at its best can offer, but are quickly turned off by the implied disapproval of their unmarried or divorced status. Classes and groups designed to help people become more welcoming need to point out the importance of not immediately asking someone where his or her spouse is. There may not be a spouse!

• **Encourage more open discussion of sexuality within your congregation.** Younger adults and older adults often do not feel the same about premarital intercourse and homosexuality. They may also not feel the same way about the nature

115

of marriage. Many of us have not seriously considered these issues, and our churches have been reluctant to discuss such potentially controversial topics.

A full consideration of these issues goes far beyond the scope of this book. We do feel, however, that it is crucial for churches to become less judgmental and more welcoming. Again, the biblical teachings about hospitality are not qualified to exclude certain categories of persons.

• **Recognize the need for variety in worship services.** For some congregations this means starting a contemporary service. For others it means integrating more contemporary elements such as hymns and drama into an existing service. Help people understand the reasons for such changes, and continue interpreting those reasons. [For more help on this, see the book ***Worship and Hospitality*** by Steve Clapp and Fred Bernhard and ***The Alternative Worship Primer*** by Cindy Hollenberg. Both are listed in the Resources and References chapter of this book.]

• **Be prepared to more quickly integrate enthusiastic young adults into the life of the church.** Don't wait until annual elections to invite people to serve on a board, commission, committee, or task force in which they are interested.

• **If your church is to be sensitive to the needs of young adults on a continuing basis, then you need to have persons of that age range as members of the major decision-making groups in your congregation.** That way their perspective is always available.

• **Recognize the reality that young adults who have not grown up in the church may not be familiar with many things the rest of us take for granted.** Note again many of the recommendations shared in the chapters on *Experiencing Hospitality in the Church* and *Welcoming Strangers*.

* **Provide many opportunities for young adults and older adults to interact with one another.** Differences in perspective are not as important when people know and like one another. Some young adults reading this book will feel that they do not have the differences in perspective that are described. Where that is the case, it is very often because healthy interactions between young adults and older adults are a regular part of the life of the congregation.

Young Adults and Church Structure

As suggested earlier, young adults are often not as patient as older adults with the slow decision-making process that dominates many of our congregations. Sharing specific models for church organization goes beyond the scope of this book, but it is crucial to recognize that truly welcoming young adults generally means moving toward a less restrictive and more permission-giving kind of church organization.

There are large numbers of older adults in most congregations who would also like to see some changes in this direction. In a congregational survey of an established midwestern congregation, people had some very strong words about the organizational structure in place at that time:

* "The organization is too top-heavy—throw it all away and we'll find out what's important."

* "I think we could get the same results with many fewer organizational-type meetings."

* "Our limited free time needs to be spent on what's really needed rather than on filling position established years ago."

* "I like this saying: 'God so loved the world that He didn't send a committee.'"

The main barrier to streamlining church organizational

117

structures and decision-making processes is that it requires a greater degree of trust. People must be willing to trust others to make decisions and to be supportive of groups with which they are not personally involved. Large congregations are more likely to have such an atmosphere because of the impossibility of a significant percentage of the membership being involved in every decision. Smaller congregations that have functioned for years with systems that required broad agreement before any change was made may find it initially difficult to let decisions be made more rapidly and by fewer people. Failure to make that transition, however, can have a very limiting effect on church growth.

Growing churches are increasingly characterized by:

• A structure that emphasizes DOING more than DECIDING. There are fewer decision-making groups and more action groups.

• A structure with fewer standing committees and more task forces or mission groups appointed as needs arise.

• A greater willingness to trust individuals and groups to make decisions without having several layers of approval.

• A clearer separation of those decisions which have significant impact on the whole congregation and need the involvement of many persons from those decisions that affect only a few people or are of relatively minor importance.

And if you come upon the perfect organizational structure for your church that pleases persons of all ages, PLEASE send the details of the structure to the authors of this book! We'd love to have it. For the present, most of us are in transition, seeking to make improvements at the pace our congregations can accept.

Hospitality and the Overlooked

> **Concept:** The congregation that takes seriously a biblical understanding of hospitality does not place restrictions on its welcome and actively seeks out those whom others might overlook.

Clarence came from a long line of relatively uneducated people who had not attended church. He didn't have any particularly negative feelings about the church, but it had never seemed relevant to his life. When his sixteen-year-old son was caught selling drugs, however, Clarence felt like his own life was coming apart. The son faced a potentially stiff jail term, and the resulting stress affected the entire family. Clarence and his wife did not see the situation in the same way and reached the point that they couldn't even talk about it with each other.

Desperate for some kind of help or perspective, Clarence decided to go to church. He came a little late, just after the announcements and the prelude, and realized, as he slipped into a pew, that he wasn't dressed as well as the others who were present. Members of the congregation sang hymns, said prayers, and greeted one another at the appropriate times. One of the hymns was vaguely familiar to Clarence, but he didn't know the others. When greetings were exchanged, he received only a weak smile and handshake from a man seated next to him.

The Scripture reading was utterly incomprehensible, and the sermon seemed full of references Clarence didn't understand: "Now this is like the story of the prodigal son. . . ." (What story of the prodigal son? And what is a prodigal?) "The atonement of Christ. . . ." (Atonement?) "The grace of God was sufficient to see her through those difficult times. . . ." (Grace? Is that the name of a person God sent to help her?)

By the time the service ended, he felt certain that he had made one of the major mistakes of his life. Whatever made him think that he could feel at home in the church? What made him think that there would be a message of hope he could understand?

Karen grew up in the church. She won prizes for her attendance at Sunday school; she sang in the children's choir; she was the president of her youth group; and she was a youth member on the church council. When she went to college, she became active in a campus ministry and went on four mission trips while an undergraduate.

She became engaged right after her graduation from college and was married in her home church with almost three hundred people in attendance. Seven years and two children later, life became increasingly confusing for Karen. She had struggled with questions of sexual orientation in both high school and college but had been taught that homosexuality was a sin and very much wanted to not be gay. She had gotten married and had children, feeling convinced that those actions would change how she felt. She loved her husband and her children, but both she and her husband increasingly realized that their relationship just wasn't working.

After a year of marital counseling, they both came to the conclusion that she was homosexual in orientation even though not in behavior. Her husband, wanting more out of marriage than she was able to give him, asked her for a divorce, and she agreed. It was a painful but peaceful splitting with an agreement to have joint custody of the children.

Karen stayed away from the church for the first two years following the divorce. She still felt guilty about her orientation and felt condemned by the anti-gay messages in the church she and her husband had been attending. She cautiously began a nonsexual relationship with a person of the same sex and feels that they may have a future together.

Not being part of a congregation felt wrong to her. She loved God deeply. She didn't understand why she was homosexual, because she sure hadn't chosen the orientation. But seven years of marriage, considerable effort on her part, and a great deal of prayer had not been able to change her orientation. She knows there are biblical passages that condemn homosexuality, but she also feels that the creation passages speak to her situation. She feels that her orientation is part of how she was created and that God has affirmed the overall goodness of life. She has increasingly begun to feel that God does accept her as she is and that the biblical passages about homosexuality, examined in their original context, are not as negative as she had been taught that they were. She has cautiously begun attending a new church, hoping that she may be able to experience enough acceptance to be honest about the struggles she is experiencing.

Nate and Taina dated each other for three years and finally decided to move into the same apartment. Nate has always been somewhat "commitment-phobic" (his words) and has generally fled relationships when the word "marriage" became too frequent a part of conversation. Taina was married right after high school and knew within two months that it had been a mistake. She stayed married, however, for four years before calling it quits because she was so concerned about what her parents and others would think of her for getting a divorce. She feels like Nate is the right person, but she is worried about his commitment-phobia and doesn't want to make a second mistake in a marriage partner. This time around, she feels like she wants a test drive before making a final commitment, which is how she sees their living with each other.

Both Nate and Taina are in their early thirties, and their faith in Christ is important to both of them. Nate, however, had not been active in a local church since he graduated from high school. Taina had been involved in a church all of her life and continued to attend following her divorce. She has told Nate that church membership and activity are very important to her.

Nate started attending worship services with Taina, and he felt warmly received by the church. Now that they have moved in with each other, however, they aren't quite sure what to say. Taina's church was very supportive of her through the divorce process, but she isn't sure how people will react to the news that she and Nate are living with each other. One of these days, their addresses in the church office will have to be changed, and they will not be able to keep their greater level of intimacy a secret.

The Gospel for All People

Churches generally succeed in growth because active members invite their friends, family members, coworkers, and neighbors to attend worship or other church events. That kind of growth is certainly consistent with an attitude of hospitality toward others, and it's only natural that the people we individually pull into the church are very often going to be those with whom we have already established relationships.

As discussed earlier in this book, however, that kind of growth tends to make for a church in which people are very much alike. Our friends, neighbors, and coworkers are generally persons who are very similar to us in at least some respects. They are generally persons of comparable income level, the same racial or ethnic background, and similar educational level. But what about those persons who are different from us in significant ways?

In **Luke 14:7–14**, Jesus describes the places of honor generally accorded others at a wedding banquet. Then our Lord suggests that those giving a lunch or dinner consider changing the guest list:

> *When you give a banquet, invite the poor, the crippled, the lame, and the blind. And you will be blessed because they cannot repay you, for you will be repaid at the resurrection of the righteous.*
> **Luke 14:13–14**

Chapter fourteen continues with Jesus telling the Parable of the Great Dinner in verses fifteen through twenty-four. In that parable, the one who held a great banquet was disappointed by the many who gave excuses and did not come. As a result, "the poor, the crippled, the lame, and the blind were invited and then people were simply drawn from the street to finish filling the places for the banquet. Jesus challenges us to reach out with hospitality to those who would otherwise stay outside the circumference of our relationships and the life of the church.

If we take that parable and the Parable of the Good Samaritan seriously, then we will find ourselves reaching out to many persons we would have otherwise overlooked. We will also find ourselves extending hospitality to those drawn to our churches even when there may be aspects of their personalities or lifestyles that make us uncomfortable. The strongest congregations have always understood and practiced that concept.

George Miller lived near Elizabethtown, Pennsylvania, from 1722 through 1798. When one of his oxen was stolen, George did not sue the person responsible because he did not want the whipping required by British law to fall on the thief. His neighbors, however, had the thief arrested.

Miller then walked twenty miles to Lancaster, Pennsylvania, where the thief was detained, to provide him with warm bedding. He demonstrated hospitality toward the thief, treating him as a friend, while his neighbors perceived the thief as an enemy. This kind of outreach in the name of Christ transforms lives and embodies the kind of peace-making to which we have all been called. [*History of the Church of the Brethren—Eastern Pennsylvania* by S.R. Zug, pp. 511–512]

Another account from Pennsylvania comes from Clyde and Emma Weaver, friends of Fred Bernhard. Emma's grandparents, who lived in Lebanon County, Pennsylvania, responded to a man who came to their door seeking help on a cold winter evening. Practicing hospitality, they gave him a meal, lodging for the night, and breakfast the next morning. They did not know him, and many people would have felt they took a significant risk.

After breakfast, their guest told them that he had just arrived from Germany and had no money to pay them. They did not expect any pay and made that clear, but their guest still wished to show his appreciation. He offered them a recipe for seasoned meat, which had been passed through his family for generations. The result of that recipe, which was not actually used in the Weaver family for many years, was what we know today as Lebanon Bologna, and it has become a popular dish in some parts of North America.

Jesse M. Burall, Fred's father-in-law, shared another account. When German POWs were incarcerated near Camp Detrick in Frederick, Maryland, the government decided to let them work during the day on area farms. Mr. Burall arranged for six of these workers, who automatically came with an armed guard.

The policy was for the prisoners to be fed lunch outside. Mr.

Burall, however, insisted that the men eat at the table with the rest of the family. This practice continued over the two-year period from 1943 to 1945. Table hospitality and prayer were always shared, and genuine friendships developed. Mr. Burall's only regret was that he couldn't get the guard to join them at the table. "Then the circle would have been completed," he said. Such outreach provides healing of relationships and natural opportunities for sharing the faith.

Compare those perspectives with our tendency today to want harsher sentences for those charged with crimes, to lock our doors to strangers, and to avoid contact with persons who represent differing ideologies.

The Overlooked

As shared at the beginning of this book, hospitality is not optional and is also not safe. The historical examples just given of persons sharing hospitality were not without risk, but people chose to act consistently with their understanding of the gospel. The authors of this book are not urging that people stop using common sense in terms of safety for themselves and others, but most of us pass up numerous opportunities to build friendships with persons who are different from us. Some of those we overlook may truly live next door to the church!

Many churches are located in neighborhoods with residents who differ in significant ways from the persons in the congregation. This is increasingly true in North America as vast numbers of persons each Sunday morning drive past many other churches to worship and learn in the church of their choice. Steve and Fred have repeatedly encountered such realities in the process of helping congregations with surveys and profiles of their membership and their ministry situations.

The following chart compares strength of agreement with two statements by members of an urban congregation with the average in other North American churches and with the average among growing congregations. The two statements were:

- Members of this church are similar in values and lifestyle to people who live immediately around the church.

- Our church is very involved with the community around the church.

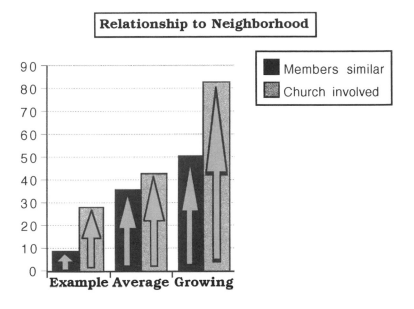

Relationship to Neighborhood

LifeQuest provided chart. Bars show the percentage agreeing or strongly agreeing with each statement.

In this particular urban congregation, fewer than 10% of the persons completing the survey felt that their members were similar in values and lifestyle to those living near the church. Fewer than 30% felt that their congregation was involved in the community around the church. There were significant racial, educational, and economic differences between church members and the neighborhood.

Those differences had begun to make members of the church feel uncomfortable coming to the church building for evening meetings and also reluctant to invite their friends to church. People in the church knew almost no one in the neighborhood. While this example represents a more extreme situation than many, it is far from unique. What would it mean for the church to move from locked doors and fearful scheduling of activities to a spirit of hospitality toward the community around the church?

It might mean:

*   Door-to-door canvassing by couples from the church to share information with people in the neighborhood about the church and to learn more about the people in that area.

*   Providing a free ice cream social for the neighborhood and encouraging all active congregational members to share in serving and visiting.

*   Surveying the neighborhood to find out what programs are needed and opening the church as appropriate to help with support groups, recreation, or other areas of need.

*   Actively inviting people in the neighborhood to attend other church activities, including worship services.

The majority of the persons who are overlooked by members of most congregations, of course, are not necessarily those in the neighborhood around the church facilities. The church should extend hospitality to all who come, including those described on the following pages. Before deciding to intentionally reach out to a particular category of persons, it's important to evaluate the extent to which the congregation as a whole is prepared to embrace those individuals. Where anxiety or fear is associated with a particular category, it may be necessary to address those feelings before taking congregational initiative to invite such persons to the church. Ignoring those feelings may do harm to both members and guests. When such persons appear at church through their own initiative or that of others, we are of course challenged to put aside our fears and follow Christ's welcoming example. Some of those who are likely to be overlooked include:

*   People whose educational level is above or below that of most in the congregation. Educational differences, similarly to financial differences, sometimes form a solid barrier to friendships. As we think about our relationships with others, we should be careful that we do not permit the fact that another person has either more or less education than ourselves to keep us from extending hospitality in the name of Christ.

- People whose economic and/or social status differs from that of most in the congregation. How many patients with no college education have considered inviting their physician to church? How many professionals have considered inviting a custodian to church? If we take the biblical concept of hospitality seriously, those differences should not keep us from extending an invitation to be part of what is valuable to us—the church.

- People who have problems with alcoholism or other forms of drug addiction. While some churches readily open their buildings for meetings by A.A. groups, most of us do not often think about inviting persons dealing with such difficulties to be part of the life of the church. Those persons, however, can gain a great deal from the Christian community; they also have rich gifts to offer us because of what they are overcoming.

- People who have been in trouble with the law and the families of those persons. The opening example of this chapter described a father affected by his son's arrest and potential imprisonment. An earlier chapter talked about the experiences of a released convict named Eddie. Our communities have ever-increasing numbers of persons who have had such experiences and who need the hospitality of Christian people.

- Victims of crime. A couple in their mid-fifties were crushed, angered, and then perplexed by the unsolved murder of their married daughter, who had been in her mid-twenties at the time of her murder near the entrance to her home. The surrounding questions and grief caused her parents to be understandably fixated on the reasons for her death and the identity of her murderer. The police explanation of "probable random violence" was not satisfactory to them. Do we let our discomfort and lack of certainty about what to say keep us from inviting and welcoming such persons?

- Unmarried persons who are living together. As

127

shared in the chapter on young adults, increasing numbers of people fall into this category. The opening of this chapter described the situation of Nate and Taina, who are wondering how they will be received when the fact that they are living with each other becomes common knowledge in the church.

Congregations differ in how they feel about couples living together and being sexually intimate before they are married. In fact there are differences of opinion within many congregations. As the practice becomes increasingly common, some Christians are rethinking their past tendency to automatically condemn such relationships. Arguing the theological issues involved in this matter goes beyond the scope of this book.

Certainly the fact that a practice is widespread does not make it "all right." Personally knowing more persons who are in such relationships or who have children in such relationships, however, may motivate many of us to think again about our beliefs and values. The majority of congregations once condemned persons who had been divorced and made them unwelcome in their sanctuaries. Today most churches, while saddened when divorce comes to its members, continue to accept persons going through such times and endeavor to be as supportive as possible. The majority of churches have people in leadership who have been divorced.

What we are arguing in this book is that the practice of hospitality needs to be extended to all persons, regardless of how we feel about their personalities, lifestyles, ethnic background, educational level, or economic status. Being an unwelcoming place to couples who are sexually intimate before marriage excludes them from the opportunity to hear the very teachings that might cause them to feel differently both about marriage and about the church. We are all seeking to grow together as disciples in Christ.

• Persons of different sexual orientation. The inclusion of this category is undoubtedly disconcerting to some. Denominations and congregations all across North

America are struggling with how to understand homosexuality in light of scientific knowledge, Scripture, and personal experience. As more and more persons of nonheterosexual orientation have become open about their feelings, the percentage of people who have a family member, friend, coworker, or neighbor who is gay, lesbian, or bisexual has continued to increase.

Arguing all the dimensions of both science and theology related to sexual orientation is a matter for an entire book. The reality is that there are many people like Karen, described in the opening to this chapter, who tried hard not to accept a homosexual orientation but who in time have concluded that such an orientation is part of their identity. Many of these are persons of deep Christian faith to whom the church is very important.

As shared in the chapter on "Welcoming Teenagers," about 10% of the youth in the typical congregation are struggling with questions of sexual orientation or have in fact concluded that they are homosexual or bisexual. These teens are already involved in the church, but many of them choose to be silent about their orientation because of fear of disapproval.

A prominent Mennonite church leader, whose name would be immediately recognized by many if we used it here, found his view of homosexuality challenged when his twenty-year-old grandson came out as gay. He described it in this way: "I've always been pretty conservative on this issue. I recognize that the Bible doesn't say a great deal about homosexuality, but what is there has always seemed to me to be prohibitive. But now I find myself with a grandson, who never wanted to be gay, who has concluded that it is part of who he is, part of how God made him. I held that little boy in my arms thirty minutes after his birth, and he has spent at least a week in my home every year of his life. I'm starting to take a new look at what the Bible says about sexuality, and I'm paying more attention to the Genesis story of creation, the context of the relatively small number of

129

prohibitions, and the strong teachings of Christ about love. I haven't sorted it all out theologically, but I have to say this: *A grandson trumps theology. You are looking at a new gay rights activist.*"

Again, the biblical admonition to show hospitality does not exclude certain categories of persons. We need to accept and love in the name of Christ all those who are open to the Christian faith. Welcoming persons is not synonymous with accepting all aspects of their lifestyle or behavior. In the midst of bitter denominational arguments about homosexuality, we need to strengthen the practice of hospitality in our congregations, embracing in love all those whom Christ brings into our lives. As we explore together what it means to be a Christian, we may find ourselves challenged and perhaps even changed in the process.

* Persons of other races or ethnic backgrounds. These individuals are very often missing from our congregations and also from our circles of friends. Tensions in public schools are frequently along racial lines. Those of us in the Christian community should be taking the initiative to extend hospitality to persons whose skin color or ancestry differs from our own.

While there is clear agreement by virtually all Christians that people of all races should be able to worship and work together in the life of the church, very few of our congregations are truly multicultural. This reality stands as a strong indictment of our inability to truly live out the Christian faith. For those wanting to do more in this area, we strongly recommend the resource **Building a Multicultural Congregation** by Edwin Bontrager (see the "Resources and References" chapter).

* Persons who are physically or mentally challenged. They not normally present in significant numbers in our congregations. Some of our churches have not eliminated the architectural barriers to persons with various physical disabilities. It's difficult to offer hospitality with our words when our physical facilities

convey something entirely different. Those who are mentally challenged may require significant adjustments by the rest of us, but their presence will generally enrich our lives. If few churches in your area are offering programs for the mentally challenged, then this could be an area for significant growth in your church. We should offer hospitality to the physically and mentally challenged, not only for their sake and because of the spirit of hospitality, but also because we have so much to learn from persons who have carried such burdens.

• Persons who are in the military and persons who are committed peace activists. Those in peace church traditions may overlook or harbor negative feelings toward those who are in the military. Persons who are opposed to military service may be overlooked by those congregations that encourage patriotism and military service. Our welcome needs to extend to persons in both categories, recognizing that Christ expects us to extend the welcome and also that we can gain from the perspective of those who differ from us.

As this book goes to press, there are deep divisions in the United States about the role this country has played with the attack of Iraq in the absence of any found weapons of mass destruction. The fear and anger from the events of September 11, 2001, fueled some support for the attacks on Afghanistan that were intended to reach those responsible for the Pentagon and World Trade Center tragedies. The military attacks on Iraq are a far more difficult matter for many people. Virtually all of our churches, however, have loved ones who serve in the military or who have family in the military, and those persons need our prayers and concern. Likewise those working for peace need our prayers and concern.

The authors of this book, both coming from peace church traditions, are not in favor of the violence that the United States unleashed on Iraq and are sickened by the number of lives which have been lost. At the same time, we have many good friends in the

131

military, and those persons see their work as contributing to a safer and more just world. We are challenged to extend hospitality and love to those with whom we agree and also to those with whom we disagree. As we approach one another with mutual respect, we learn from each other and find our perspectives both challenged and at times transformed.

Obviously the listing could be extended for many additional pages. We refer those wanting to know more on this topic to helpful chapters in Steve Clapp and Sam Detwiler's book **Sharing Living Water**.

Remember that many of the categories shared in this chapter bring us into connection with persons who may make us feel uncomfortable or with whom we may have serious disagreements. The essence of hospitality, however, focuses on the obligations of the host rather than those of the guest.

Servant Evangelism

John, a man in his early fifties who was extremely active in a local congregation, shared these words with one of the authors of this book:

> I got very turned off toward God and the church by things that happened when I was a child. Sunday school seemed to me way too strict, and my father would whip me if I complained too much about having to go. In my mind I formed this image of God as a very bad tempered, demanding dictator. I wasn't sure if he was real or not, but if he was, I sure didn't want any part of him. After I got out of high school, I refused to go to church for anything except weddings and funerals.
>
> When I was in my late twenties, my wife and I moved to this community. Our second child was born to us that year. My wife wanted us to attend a church, but I wanted no part of it.

We got started doing volunteer work in this soup kitchen downtown. We volunteered on Mondays, the same day that three people from a small congregation were all there helping. One of them was a man in his seventies, and he was very impressive because of the compassion he showed for the people we served and because of the interest he took in each of us. Over a period of time, I found myself feeling open to Christ again because of his influence. While he stood out, the other two were also kind and obviously didn't believe that God was a heavenly tyrant.

We didn't join the church those people were from, but they are the reason that my faith was renewed and that my family returned to church.

Words are powerful, and the right words, sincerely shared, have helped bring many people to faith in Christ and involvement in a local church. Many excellent books and reports on faith sharing and invitational evangelism have helped people more effectively use words to communicate their faith in Christ and their love for the church.

In a movement that is sweeping the country, more and more Christian people are seeking to share their faith not just in words but in actions of service and concern toward others. This **servant evangelism** movement is consistent with the Gospel; and, measured in very pragmatic terms, it works! Many people, like John, have been turned off toward Christ and the church because of unpleasant experiences, the negative influence of another person, or the contradiction between what some Christians claim to believe and how they actually live.

Sincere acts of service, like the work performed in the soup kitchen, cause people to think about Christians and the church in different ways. The words shared by the man in his seventies and by the other two from that church had impact on John and his wife because of the actions that accompanied the words.

Hospitality certainly impacts how we respond to those persons who visit our congregations for worship and other activities. True hospitality, however, also affects how we respond to persons in the community who may or may not have any openness whatsoever toward the church.

133

About 95% of adults in the United States say in response to Gallup and other opinion polls that they do believe in God, but on a typical Sunday morning no more than 40% of the population is in church. Percentages of belief and of church involvement run lower in Canada. Some persons claim affiliation with a congregation but rarely attend, and others refuse to be members.

Our outreach as Christians and active church members has been hindered by our difficulty in realistically viewing persons outside the church. Our default thinking is too often that those outside the church do not believe in God and are not involved in acts of service toward others. This is not true.

While many persons outside of the church may verbalize their faith in different ways than those of us in the church, the majority of them do have faith in God. Vast numbers are also quick to help persons in need and to affiliate with service organizations. As churches, we have often done an inadequate job helping those outside the church recognize that church involvement:

- can help them deepen their relationship with God.

- can offer them meaningful community, which will improve the quality of their lives.

- can give them opportunities to work with others to improve life for those who are less fortunate.

Servant evangelism seeks to share the faith by acts of love, compassion, forgiveness, and acceptance toward others. Those acts create opportunities for us to verbally share what we believe and to help pull people into the family of God.

Maintenance of the institutional church has become such an overwhelming need in many of our traditions that we tend to think about service to Christ consisting of:

- serving on a board or committee.

- teaching a Sunday school class.

134

- painting, renovating, or decorating some part of the church facilities.

- witnessing to the faith and inviting others to worship services to strengthen the congregation.

- giving generously of our money to the needs of the local church and, to some extent, to outreach needs through the church budget.

But many individual Christians and many congregations are recognizing that those forms of service are not the only ones to which our Lord may be calling us. People are finding meaningful opportunities for service in:

- working with food banks, soup kitchens, homeless shelters, and other programs to serve the needy.

- witnessing to their faith by providing child care for single parents, support groups for those who are grieving, and mentoring for those in trouble with the law.

- making the community aware of their church's presence through free photographs of children, the distribution of devotional booklets, and gift-wrapping at Christmas.

When we think about servant evangelism, we are expanding the parameters of our service to Christ from the needs of the church as an institution to the needs of the community as a whole and of the world to which we all belong.

The Benedictine Legacy

Centuries ago the Benedictines began practicing biblical hospitality to strangers without knowing or caring about the background of those persons. Monasteries were situated in towns and the country as common places where hospitality could be found. The Rule of St. Benedict was given sometime between 530 and 543 A.D. and is still known and practiced:

135

> *Let all the guests that come be received like Christ himself, for he will say: "I was a stranger and ye took me in"* [*Commentary on the Rule of St. Benedict* by Paul Delatte, p. 330].

These guests were considered so important that the Superior was even ordered to break his fast for the sake of the guest, unless it was a principal fast day.

The guests represented Christ, so the monks did all that they could to see that each person was treated as though Christ were present in that individual. They provided for both the temporal and spiritual needs of guests. Such a standard would greatly increase our personal welcomes to the strangers we encounter and also the welcome of our congregations to those who are too often overlooked.

How Welcoming are Your Physical Facilities?

Concept: The church's physical facilities can be part of your congregation's welcome or can be a barrier to participation by members and visitors.

"I sure feel ashamed of myself for all the times I said we didn't need a wheelchair ramp or an elevator," Howard gasped to his wife as he used the railing to help pull himself up the steps from the church basement to the main floor.

"Don't you think you should rest a few minutes before going the rest of the way?" his wife Martha asked.

"Can't risk the loss of momentum. I'll be okay," but his voice didn't sound reassuring to himself or to Martha. Since a triple-bypass surgery nine months earlier, Howard continued to feel like everything took three times as much energy as it should. The surgeon had told him that it would take six months for him to resume normal activity, but Howard felt more like it would be six years, if ever.

"I still think we should ask them to move the class to one of the first floor rooms," Martha said as she took Howard's arm to offer him some support. He didn't jerk his arm away from her and make his frequent snorting noise, which told her that he was indeed feeling drained.

"But there really isn't another classroom upstairs that's available. What would they do, make the Happy Days class change to the basement? Those people are older than I am. I think you have to have arthritis, diabetes, or heart disease to be a member of the class."

"Howard," Martha scolded, "you know better than to talk that way."

He sighed as he paused for a moment a third of the way from the top of the stairs. "I sure do," he agreed. "The truth of the matter is that most of the people in that class are in better shape than I am. Maybe we should ask them to trade rooms."

While Howard and Martha were making their way up the stairs, Paul and Jane, a very healthy young adult couple, were getting ready to visit another congregation on the opposite side of town. They were driving around First Church's block for the third time. "I really think it's okay to park in the restaurant's lot," Jane offered to her husband for the second time. "The restaurant looks like it's closed and there are a few cars there already. Those must be people going to church."

"But if you're wrong, they're going to tow the car. That sign looks pretty explicit and doesn't say that Sunday is an exception," her husband Paul responded. "We saw a lot of people parking a couple of blocks down the street and walking. I think that's what people do when the lot by the church gets full."

"We could just keep driving around the block for another hour or so," Jane suggested, "and then the service would be over."

Paul laughed at her comment and at himself. "You're right," he admitted as he pulled into the restaurant's parking lot. "We're going to need time anyway to figure out which door to go in. There must be five entrances, and we've seen people use all of them except the big doors that look like they'd lead to the sanctuary."

"But I think that's just like my home church," said Jane. "Because there's no parking right in front of the sanctuary, no one ever enters that way. Sometimes they even forget to unlock those doors."

"Well, this church is even bigger than yours. We'll be lost for sure if we go in the wrong door." They got out of their car and headed toward the church.

In another church in the same community, Betty and Sarah

138

were visiting with each other as they washed their hands in the women's restroom. Sarah and Betty were both single parents who worked for the same company. Sarah had belonged to the congregation for seven years, and Betty was there as Sarah's guest. Betty didn't have a church home and had talked with Sarah after work about feeling an emptiness in her life. Sarah had suggested that Betty and her young child attend church that weekend.

Betty, however, already had a couple of concerns, which she began expressing as she pulled paper towels out of the dispenser. "Sarah, has the paint around the baseboard in here been peeling for a long time?"

"Peeling?" Sarah looked at the baseboard. "It is peeling, isn't it? I've never noticed that before. It probably hasn't been peeling for too long."

"I don't want to make a big deal out of it," Betty said as her face flushed slightly. "It's just that it would make me nervous to have Kimberly in here with us. My child will put anything that fits into her mouth. It would be just like her to chew on that paint because the color is neat."

"Yuck!" Sarah made a face. "That doesn't help us make a good impression, does it?"

"I don't mean that I'm rejecting your church because some paint is peeling," Betty said. "It's just that the peeling paint on top of how crowded the nursery room looked made me wonder if your church has been able to handle the fast growth it's been experiencing."

Underestimating the Message of the Facilities

We can too easily grow comfortable with aspects of our physical facilities that really aren't welcoming. Betty observed the peeling paint in the restroom right away and was concerned about it as a potential hazard to children, but Sarah had not noticed it. In that particular congregation, the paint had in fact been peeling for about two years. Our physical facilities do communicate a message to members and visitors. We want that message to be consistent with what we are attempting to communicate through our words to people.

Lack of attention to physical facilities can especially be a problem for those of us in traditions that emphasize simple lifestyles and who don't want to go overboard in what we spend on the building and grounds. Think about the barriers or potential barriers experienced by the persons at the beginning of this chapter:

- Stairs and steep inclines can be significant problems for persons in wheelchairs, for persons with arthritis, and for persons with conditions such as heart disease, emphysema, and severe asthma.

- Unclear parking instructions can leave people in a state of confusion. The restaurant parking lot near First Church was in fact available to church members and visitors on Sunday mornings and also on weekday evenings, but the sign didn't say so. An arrangement with the restaurant to include a sign about Sunday and evening parking would have ended some confusion. A system of parking ushers or greeters can also provide a means to help people deal with limited parking— or simply to help them feel at home when they arrive.

- Not knowing which door to use for a church can be frustrating to those who have not attended before. Churches that have multiple entrances need to have signs that make it clear which entrances are for the sanctuary, for education, and for church offices.

- Betty had the impression that the nursery in Sarah's church was crowded. While a church that feels comfortably full and busy can convey a sense of enthusiasm and energy, no one wants to feel confined. And a crowded nursery is a little disturbing! People also do not want to be forced into too close a proximity to other persons during worship, classes, or fellowship times. People are reluctant to linger and visit if the narthex area of the sanctuary is always jammed.

- Although people often do not think to verbalize that the church's physical facilities appear well maintained, that in fact is an expectation that almost everyone has. People don't want to see peeling paint where children might eat it, as was the case in Sarah's church. They also don't want to see peeling paint on the outside of the church or in any other place. They don't want to find cracks in the sidewalks or the stairs that are big enough to be dangerous. They also expect the church grounds to be clean, well-trimmed, and attractive.

The church is not a building. We know that. But one or more buildings house the majority of our church services and programs. The welcome communicated by those facilities needs to be just as positive as that communicated by the words of the pastor, other church staff, and members.

A Checklist on Physical Facilities

Check as many of the following statements as apply to the physical facilities of your congregation. Items you check merit further evaluation by appropriate groups in the congregation.

_____ **Our sanctuary seats far more people than our average worship attendance.** While people don't want to be crowded, they also feel strange if sitting too far away from other worshipers. They are not likely to greet or be greeted by persons not sitting near them. If your sanctuary seems to be swallowing your congregation, encourage people to sit more toward the front of the sanctuary or consider meeting in another part of the church. A change of location works especially well for a contemporary service. Some churches take out a few rows of pews and change the spacing of the remaining pews.

_____ **Our sanctuary is 80% or more full at most worship services.** If that's the case, then you may be getting close to a leveling off of worship attendance. People in general seem reluctant to sit in a sanctuary that is completely full. Many people today are also not as willing as past generations to sit in close proximity to others and absolutely do not want to have

141

their bodies physically touching anyone who is not a member of the family. Some older sanctuaries that were once intended to seat, for example, 400 people may by today's standards only provide truly comfortable seating for 320. You may need to consider expanded physical facilities or a move to an additional service of worship.

_____ **Our sanctuary doesn't provide an especially attractive setting for worship.** This generally means there's nothing wrong with the sanctuary but also nothing unique or uplifting about it. Unless you are part of a religious tradition that places great emphasis on simplicity in worship, you may wish to consider what might be done to increase the beauty and warmth of the sanctuary. That could include new altar and pulpit coverings (paraments) if appropriate to your tradition, stained glass windows, new pews, refinishing existing pews, replacing pews with chairs, repainting, or other improvements. Remember, as in one's own home, it isn't always the amount of money spent on furnishings so much as the feeling of warmth conveyed by the colors and textures that are present. Persons with a background in interior design can often be a significant help even if they are not experienced in church interiors.

_____ **Our sanctuary and other facilities aren't especially "child friendly."** If children spill something on a pew, chair, or the floor, does it create a significant problem? If so, as opportunities arise, try to increase the comfort level for children and their parents. Use stain-resistant fabrics and surfaces wherever possible. Carpeting in children's classrooms provides a comfortable surface, and children can enjoy sitting on the floor for some activities—but be sure the carpeting is clean and attractive!

_____ **Altar furnishings in our sanctuary cannot be arranged to accommodate drama or other innovations in worship.** This can make it difficult to experiment with more contemporary forms of worship. There may be limits on what can be done about this unless the altar furnishings are showing age and replacement would be logical. If your church decides to start a separate contemporary service, then one option may be to hold that service in another part of the church building. Some congregations that have sanctuaries much larger than needed for the average worship attendance have taken out a few pews or rows of chairs near the front to make more flexible space available.

If your church wants to get serious about more contemporary worship, you may need to consider a task force for the purpose of evaluating your physical facilities. It may be time for the sanctuary to be renovated to make it more flexible. Such task forces often visit the sanctuaries of other congregations to get ideas on how they might proceed. See our book *Worship and Hospitality* or the book *Alternative Worship Primer* by Cindy Hollenberg.

_____ **The speaker system in our sanctuary doesn't work well, and a hearing-impaired person would have problems knowing what is happening.** If that's the case, then you should investigate upgrading that system. People develop hearing problems for a number of reasons but are especially likely to experience difficulties with advancing age. Given the increasing percentage of the population in North America that is over the age of sixty-five, needs in this area will continue to increase. Our worship settings should be ones in which persons with impaired hearing feel comfortable. That generally means a good speaker system and special units for those who need extra enhancement. Deaf persons, of course, can benefit from signing; increasing numbers of congregations are making that available.

_____ **We couldn't add classes or groups without expanding our Christian education facilities.** If that is the case, then it's time to take a careful look at available space. Classes and small groups are among the very best ways to help new persons feel welcomed into the life of the congregation and to give those persons opportunity to build relationships with others. It's often easier to accomplish growth by adding class and group opportunities than by trying to increase the numbers in existing groups. Dividing some existing rooms, experimenting with additional times for classes or groups, and other strategies may be alternatives to construction. At a certain point, however, building more space may be absolutely critical.

As discussed in an earlier chapter, some congregations have been moving a significant amount of their Christian education activities to a weekday evening (generally Wednesday) or to Sunday evening. Sometimes that strategy can take pressure off in terms of educational space, but the most successful of these programs can in fact tax existing facilities!

_____ **Our Christian education classrooms can't really be described as comfortable and attractive.** If they aren't, then do something about it! They are part of the welcome of your church to present members and to potential members. Some churches spend enormous amounts of money on attractive worship settings but almost completely neglect Christian education facilities. Rooms need to feel bright, warm, and welcoming. Chairs need to be comfortable and of appropriate size for the age level. Carpeting can be a pleasant touch in any classroom but should be stain resistant.

_____ **We do not have a comfortable and attractive area for youth to meet.** If that's the case, then you need to involve the young people themselves in the process of upgrading one or more meeting areas. Remember that what is comfortable and welcoming to teenagers may not always be what adults would choose! Many youth, for example, appreciate having an entire wall which is painted white and on which people can feel free to write, draw, or paint whatever they want. Consider having a small area for food preparation where the youth meet to save extra movement and also to eliminate the problem of needing to leave the church kitchen absolutely spotless in order to avoid getting in trouble!

A good sound system linked to a CD player, television, and DVD player can be a significant help with programming and also an asset for recreational times. Some churches place computers with Internet connections where youth meet both because of the programming potential and because some youth may not have computer access at home and would benefit from computer availability at the church. If you do this, be sure to utilize a software program that restricts access to pornographic sites!

_____ **We do not have all the ramps, elevators, and/or other accommodations needed for persons with physical disabilities and other mobility or energy limitations to use our facilities.** Making these changes can be an expensive process, and some churches are tempted not to do so on the basis that "No one who needs a ramp or elevator is coming to our church right now." As discussed in the chapter *Hospitality and the Overlooked*, such persons are also not likely to start coming unless the accommodations to their needs have been met. There's nothing more unwelcoming than discovering that you can't even get inside a building without the help of one or more other persons. Even if your congregation lacks persons who are restricted to wheelchairs or crutches, you almost certainly have people who suffer from other conditions who can benefit from a reduction in the number of stairs with which they must cope.

_____ **We need more parking for our congregation.** If so, start developing a strategy for expanding your current parking. That could include asking a nearby business for permission to use its lot when the business is closed and offering to pay for a sign to that effect. It could include utilizing parking ushers or greeters to watch for people who need help finding a parking space. It could include acquiring more property for an expanded or additional parking lot. Hospitality includes not expecting people to walk too far in order to attend church events. Having to park five blocks away isn't reasonable.

_____ **We have plenty of parking, but it isn't paved. We simply park in a dirt or grass lot adjacent to the church.** If that's the case, then you need to consider paving that lot. When it rains, people get their shoes covered with mud if they have to walk through a grass or dirt parking lot. That doesn't make people feel they've been warmly welcomed by the congregation. A family visiting a congregation in eastern Pennsylvania returned from the worship service to discover that their car had sunk a couple of inches into the grass-covered lot following a heavy rain. The husband and teenage son both became covered with mud as they pushed the car free. Though they laughed about the incident at the time, they did not return to that congregation.

_____ **The narthex area or entrance to the sanctuary is fairly small and doesn't encourage visiting by those who come.** If this is the case, give careful study to strategies for improvement, including the possible elimination of some pews at the back of the sanctuary or an expansion by construction. The time just before and just after a worship service is a prime opportunity for people to visit with one another. You want a physical setting that encourages those interchanges to take place. Churches that are arranged so that their coffee or fellowship time can be held in the narthex or adjacent to it have larger percentages of individuals stay for that time and mix with one another as a result.

_____ **Our church office facilities feel crowded and/or aren't especially attractive.** The church office is the setting in which many persons experience the hospitality of the church. If the office is too small and feels crowded, people feel uncomfortable and won't stay long. While it may sometimes feel desirable to a busy church secretary or pastor to have people stay only briefly, that isn't the overall impression the church wants to give.

Some churches provide comfortable chairs or a small lounge area just outside the office so that people can wait comfortably to see the pastor without necessarily being engaged in a lengthy conversation with a secretary who is trying desperately to complete the newsletter or bulletin! The office of the pastor or of any other professional staff member should be attractive and comfortable. You want that space to create a warm, safe feeling that will encourage people to be open and honest in their sharing.

You also want the office to include well-maintained, current equipment to help the secretary, pastor, and any other staff members do their work efficiently and comfortably. Equipment that produces sloppy-looking newsletters and bulletins conveys to people that the church doesn't take these matters seriously. Attractive materials convey the hospitality of the congregation.

_____ **It's actually a little difficult to find our church if one isn't familiar with the community.** If this is the case, then you need to invest in signs that can help people locate your building. In fact, you need signs showing the way to your church even if it is easy to find! You also need a sign on the church building or in front of the church building that clearly identifies it! Some churches simply assume that everyone will know their name without the necessity of its appearing prominently on the building itself. That's not the kind of welcoming spirit the church wants to convey.

Some churches experience difficulty with city regulations in terms of the posting of signs. Getting permission to display signs giving directions to the church may require some interpretation to those in the city with authority over these matters or in some cases appeal to a city council or planning board. Another alternative can be to seek permission from property owners to put signs on their property. Many businesses and homeowners are willing to give that permission for churches.

_____ **Our church building(s) and grounds don't stand out as especially attractive or inviting.** If that's the case, then it's time for work to be done! The building needs to communicate that the body of Christ takes pride in the place where it gathers and welcomes others who wish to share in its activities.

Churches often overlook the value of landscaping to the appearance of the facilities. Consider these possibilities:

*   Display a Peace Pole near the entrance to the church. There is a Peace Pole movement around North America. A Peace Pole generally proclaims "May peace prevail on earth" in four or more different languages. You can find further information on the Internet at http://www.world-peace.org/peacepoles.html.

*   Some churches provide a "Meditation Garden" or a "Peace Garden," that has flowers, plants, and benches for sitting and reflecting. This can be a wonderful project for persons in your congregation who have green thumbs and derive considerable pleasure from gardening. Some churches go so far as to label the flowers and plants for the benefit of those visiting the garden, and others have a covered container to hold devotional materials that people can read while in the garden.

*   If appropriate to your climate, flowers near the entrances to the church convey a strong message of welcome.

*   Many churches need to thin out landscaping that has grown out of control over the years. New landscaping can make an enormous difference in the appearance of your church.

*   Also consider the role that flowers and plants may play on the inside of your church! Many churches use fresh flowers on the altar for worship, but not so many consider the fact that flowers and plants can add to the warmth throughout the physical facilities.

The preceding checklist, of course, is not exhaustive. We do hope it will encourage you to think with greater intentionality about what is communicated by your church building(s) and grounds. Just as our residences communicate something of our values and personalities, so also do our church buildings convey a sense of the values and personality of the congregation. Be sure the message is one of welcome!

The Changing Shape
of Worship and Program

> **Concept:** We should continually strive to make the
> services and programs of the church expressions of
> the welcome we want extended to all people.

As the increasing pace of change affects every aspect of
society, we can't escape continually examining the routines,
procedures, and practices that are part of the Christian
community. The church that takes seriously the provision of
hospitality to its members and to visitors will stay alert for ways
to further widen the welcome it offers. In this chapter we share
some further thoughts that may be helpful in your congregation's outreach.

Creating Comfort in Worship

As soon as the organ began, Maxine realized that she had
misread the hymn number in the bulletin. She was on 588, but
it didn't appear that anyone else was. She had to get very close
to the man on her right in order to see what hymn number had
been chosen. 533. The threes had appeared as eights to her.
Why did the bulletin have to be in such small type? Even with
trifocals, she just couldn't make sense of letters and numbers in
small print.

And Maxine is hardly alone. Many people, of various ages,
have difficulty reading small print. Even books like this one, for
reasons of economy, tend to be printed in a smaller typeface
than is comfortable reading for many people. When printing
thousands of copies of a book, a difference in type size can make
a significant difference in the cost of the finished product. That's
not normally the case with bulletins for Sunday morning. Even

if larger sheets of paper must be used to accommodate a larger type size in the bulletin, the additional cost is not high compared to the benefits it brings to many people. Some churches provide special large print bulletins for those with difficulty seeing, but that solution has two problems. First, it doesn't benefit guests who often have no idea that the larger size is available. Second, it makes people feel self-conscious about their vision problems. If the print is larger and bolder for everyone, no one has to feel singled out.

Everything about the bulletin should be prepared with the guest in mind. For example:

- The bulletin itself should extend a prominent welcome. It should be clear that guests are expected!

- If the bulletin contains something like a *Doxology* or the *Gloria Patri*, a hymn number or the words should be provided. Guests should not be expected to be familiar with such traditions.

- If the Lord's Prayer is used, then people should at least be informed whether sins, debts, or trespasses is the wording used. A simple parenthesis after "The Lord's Prayer" indication in the bulletin can provide the word. Some congregations choose to print out the full wording to the prayer.

- No steps or responses should be taken for granted. The bulletin should include all the information needed for the service.

- Special instructions such as whether or not guests can share in communion should be included in the bulletin.

Pastors and other worship leaders likewise want to continually keep the guest in mind in directing the service, being careful not to make assumptions. As pointed out in the checklist in the chapter *Welcoming Strangers*, those who share announcements and joys and concerns should be sure to introduce themselves and to speak in such a way that guests will not feel excluded. Announcements that pertain to only a few people should generally not be made during the worship service.

Many pastors have learned that giving a brief introduction to a passage of Scripture often helps not only guests but also long-time members gain more from the biblical reading. Pastors who are sensitive to guests are careful to preach in a way that avoids theological jargon that may be unfamiliar to persons who have not been previously active in the life of a church.

The development of a complete theology of worship goes considerably beyond the scope of this book and the space available for this chapter. It is important, however, to stay aware of the tremendous diversity people feel about what constitutes meaningful worship. Traditional hymns and organ music are on target for large numbers of persons who have been raised in the church, but there are growing numbers of people who appreciate more contemporary forms of music. Some churches have sub-stantial numbers of people who like country western and even Christian rock. Contemporary Christian hymns, such as those by Michael W. Smith, have gained significant acceptance in many congregations. Practicing hospitality means having appre-ciation for the wide range of what speaks to people and enables their ability to offer meaningful worship to God. The following statements came out of a single congregation of 137 people:

- "I liked it on Youth Sunday when some of the young people played CDs and tapes of songs they especially liked. I thought one of the songs by Tori Amos was wonderful."

- "I can't believe the pastor let the teenagers play some of that music in worship. That song by Tori Amos was the limit for me. Why can't we all agree on some of the great music by people like Charles Wesley and Fannie Crosby?"

- "I listen to country western music all the time in the car. Why can't we have some music in the church that's similar? The classical music and the organ may speak to some people, but the words don't mean a thing to me and the organ grates on my ear."

- "I have tried, but I simply cannot understand the fascination with contemporary Christian music. Our choir and some of the soloists keep doing

151

things by Sandi Patti. But have they paid any attention to the words? All that music seems so shallow to me."

• "I find so much meaning in some of the music of Sandi Patti that we've been doing. She went through some hard times a few years ago, and it changed what she sings, or at least I think so."

• "We are so fortunate to have a good organ and such a skilled organist. I remain seated in the sanctuary to listen to the postlude. She plays a lot of Bach, and those works lift my spirits and give me energy."

• "I can appreciate some of the more contemporary hymns and anthems we've been using, but I have to admit that the traditional songs are the ones which speak to me at the deepest levels. We have to include both kinds in the service."

We could keep providing quotes from that congregation, but you can already see the trend—diversity in what gives meaning to people!

Of course that's just talking about music, not about other aspects of worship, such as the use of drama or video instead of a sermon as discussed in earlier chapters. It seems increasingly impossible to have "a" service that will appeal to all age groups and interests. Some pastors feel like the only place they have achieved unity in worship is in uniting people in their conclusion that their needs are not being met!

Looking at worship through the lens of hospitality, however, should change our perspective. In terms of hospitality, our focus is not simply or even primarily on meeting our own needs. We want to meet the needs of others and especially of those who are strangers to us! We are the hosts and want the service to be meaningful to our guests.

That kind of switch in attitude can move a congregation in two different directions, depending on the size and resources of the church:

1. Churches that focus on hospitality find a greater acceptance of diversity within existing services of worship, with people recognizing that the needs of others should be met—and especially the needs of those who are guests and who may have been turned off by past experiences with worship.

2. Churches that focus on hospitality and have the needed resources in leadership, settings, and membership may create different types of services. Many will have a traditional service and a contemporary service. Some may choose to offer even greater variety such as: a small communion service, a traditional service, a contemporary service led by youth, and a service with gospel and country western music.

Offering variety in the services helps existing members by letting them select the style that speaks most effectively to them. The variety also serves prospective members, our guests, by giving them the opportunity to experience more than a single style of worship. The nontraditional opportunities are especially valuable to those persons who did not grow up in the church and thus have no substantial past history of a traditional style of worship.

We sometimes forget that there are different benefits to worship services that are relatively small in number and to those that are relatively large. In fact, some very large churches have chosen to create worship experiences that are likely to draw relatively small attendance because of the timing or location of the service. That might include an early morning service or a service in a small chapel rather than the sanctuary.

There are persons in our society who are very uncomfortable in large groups. Those persons will often find a service with an average attendance in the range of thirty to eighty more attractive than one with an average attendance in the hundreds or even thousands. There are fewer persons with whom they need to interact, and the setting feels less threatening.

Of course worshiping with a small group, especially with as few as twenty or thirty people, may be quite uncomfortable for others. Some persons truly like to become lost in the crowd!

They fear being put on the spot and would prefer slipping into the service and then slipping out. While we need to take steps to be sure we eventually become acquainted with such persons, we also need to respect their desire for a greater amount of privacy than we ourselves may feel.

Every congregation has limitations on the options that can be offered either in a single worship service or in multiple services. Looking at worship from the standpoint of hospitality, however, should enable us to focus more on the needs of others and less on our own needs. That doesn't mean that our own needs shouldn't be met in the service, but it does mean that we have the ability and desire to take a broader look, to care about meeting the needs of others.

A Caution

Having talked about the differences in our view of worship that come when we are concerned about the needs of our guests, one caution needs to be shared. **Worship is above all the offering we make to God and the celebration of God's love.** In the worship setting, as in other settings in the church, we keep before us the need to show hospitality to others, but God is the ultimate focus.

We don't want to become so obsessed with offering endless variety to meet the needs of ourselves and others that we fail to recognize that our creator is the object of our worship. We don't want to make our own needs or the needs of others into idols we worship instead of God. That's not an argument against diversity in worship. In fact seeing God as the focus of worship is actually liberating, for God clearly can and does accept worship in a multitude of forms. The danger is that we can let the forms become the object of worship rather than the means of worship.

In *The Screwtape Letters*, C.S. Lewis, writing fictional words of advice from the demon Screwtape to his nephew Wormwood, points out that the devil's needs can be well met by encouraging people to keep searching for the ideal church:

> *Surely you know that if a man can't be cured of churchgoing, the next best thing is to send him all over the city looking for the church that "suits" him*

154

until he becomes a taster or connoisseur of church-es. . . . The search for a "suitable" church makes the man a critic where the Enemy wants him to be a pupil [Tarrytown, NY; Spire Books edition © 1976, p. 81].

The "enemy" from the perspective of the demon is, of course, God. If sending people on a search for a "suitable" church is one of the strategies of contemporary demons, it is a strategy that has been successful in many ways! More and more people who move into a new community do shop for the church that feels best relative to their needs. Decreases in denominational loyalty over the last two decades have fueled the church-shopping mentality.

The purpose of greater variety in worship that we are advocating in this book isn't primarily to make our congregations competitive in a church-shopping market. The purpose is to make our congregations more genuinely welcoming by showing concern for the outward forms that will best enable people to connect with Jesus Christ. The result may be beneficial to us in terms of competition with other congregations, but that is not the purpose of the changes. The distinction seems to us an important one.

We invite you to explore these matters further in our book **Worship and Hospitality,** which includes chapters on:

- Hospitality as a lens for viewing worship
- Changing paradigms in worship
- How hospitality should affect our view of church music
- How the setting for worship reflects hospitality (or not!)
- How congregational hospitality can come through in worship
- The importance of the flow of the service
- How to take a fresh look at the role of the sermon
- Understanding the evangelistic potential of worship while recognizing that evangelism is not the central purpose of worship
- A study guide for individual or group use
- Resources for people wanting to know more

Baptism and Church Membership

In the spirit of hospitality, we need to be aware that our traditional style of public baptism and statement of membership vows in front of the entire congregation may pose a barrier for some persons. These are likely to be individuals who are not comfortable with large groups of people. This is especially the case for those denominational traditions that baptize only by immersion. Some people are terrified to be baptized by immersion in front of a large gathering. This is not an issue of their commitment to Christ or to the church but rather of their own mental health and well-being.

Some churches find it theologically impossible to handle baptism and member confirmation in any setting other than the regular congregational worship services. If that is one's position, obviously innovation in this area is not an option. If your theological perspective, however, gives room for a recognition of the psychological barriers present for a minority of people, there are some alternatives.

Consider the option of a semi-private baptism and/or confirmation service during the week or on a Sunday afternoon with immediate family, a deacon (if appropriate in your tradition), a board representative, and the pastor present. Public recognition can be given the following Sunday as people are introduced to the congregation and given membership materials either by their coming to the front of the church or by their standing briefly in the congregation. That kind of public acknowledgment is far less threatening to some persons than public baptism and repetition of vows.

Another alternative is to offer the semi-private service either right before or right after regular congregational worship. Some churches like to do so right after worship because that gives the opportunity for those who are moved to a decision during the worship service to make an immediate response.

Complex theological views and local church traditions clearly impact what can be done in this area. Our encouragement to you is to reflect on what it means to offer hospitality to those whose emotional well-being affects their comfort in public settings.

Prayer and Prayer Rooms

Like most congregations, the Oakland Church recognized that it could benefit from a great deal more prayer and a great deal less gossip! In reflecting on ways to encourage more prayer among those who were members and also seeking ways to respond to guests who might find themselves especially moved, the church decided to establish a prayer room.

The prayer room offers comfortable furniture, warm lighting, and reading material about the spiritual life. At the end of each worship service, those who wish are invited to go to the prayer room, located near the sanctuary, where volunteers are present. The volunteers are there to answer questions and respond to the needs of those who come. This provides a setting for persons who feel a need for personal sharing or further prayer at the end of worship. This can include people who are ready to profess their faith in Christ, people who are dealing with the serious illness of a loved one, and people who find themselves with unanswered questions at the end of the service.

The prayer room also finds use during the week as people enter it to pray privately and to examine the resources found there. People have a hunger for prayer and for an overall deepening of the spiritual life, and the presence of the prayer room has become an outward sign of the importance of the spiritual life to the congregation. It in no way is a substitute for the kind of sharing and growing that occurs in organized classes and groups, but it is a response to the deep-seated need for personal prayer that exists in all of us.

Listening as Vital to Hospitality and Program

"To be perfectly candid," Helen shared with Beth, "I've been looking for a church that has a good group for single parents. I liked worshiping at your church last week, and I'm enjoying our lunch—but I feel the need to be part of a group of single parents rather than trying to fit in with a class filled with married couples or one with singles who have no children." Beth had met Helen the previous Sunday and had invited her to share lunch on Tuesday. The conversation about the church had been positive, but here was a significant need that the church wasn't meeting.

157

"I can sure understand that," replied Beth. "As I shared earlier, I was a single parent for almost four years. A group like that would have been a big help to me then. Actually we have at least three or four single parents in the church right now. What I wonder is if we couldn't get a group like that started."

"That sounds good, but I feel like I need a group now rather than a year from now. Some of us talked about a singles group in the church I was in before moving here, but the idea rusted on the agenda of the board."

"I understand, but it doesn't take us a year to start something new in our church. Our pastor and the board actively encourage people to do things to improve the church and its opportunities for people. Would you be willing to help start a new group?"

"Sure, but I'm brand new. Would people pay any attention to me?"

"Yes, they would. New people sometimes have the best ideas and the greatest enthusiasm. Tom Evans, the chairperson of our board, just joined the church two years ago. I'd also be glad to help get something started. If we talk to Pastor Jim and to Tom, they'll have more ideas on how to make something happen. We may already have more single parents than I know about, and there have to be others near the church. Why don't we see what's possible?"

They did. The result was not only that Helen joined the church but also that a single parents group started meeting before she had even transferred her membership. That was a congregation that took hospitality seriously and also believed in enabling ministries to happen.

Helen and Beth are part of a church on the east coast, but their experience could have happened at the Oakland Church. The Oakland Church's focus on hospitality has resulted in a greatly increased emphasis on listening to the needs of people— those already in the church and those interested in the church. The prayer room was a direct outgrowth of that listening.

Much church programming in the past at Oakland, as in many other congregations, has consisted of a few leaders identifying an area for emphasis and then "selling" the idea to the congregation. Such an approach can have good results if the programs are on target with the needs of many in the church, but people rarely have the enthusiasm for the ideas of others that they have for their own ideas!

Dynamic churches today increasingly have programs and opportunities generated by persons in the congregation, based on the needs, interests, and gifts of those persons. Such churches extend to people considerable freedom to move ahead with new program ideas. That may happen through the creation of a mission group or task force rather than through an existing commission or committee.

Congregations need to be guided by an overall vision and mission. The vision and mission, however, need to be broad enough that the respective callings that people experience can become part of it. The new people who become part of the church, like Helen, may be the ones who start important new ministries.

The way that programming happens in churches around the country is being transformed. An understanding of hospitality can enrich the existing programs of your congregation and also result in significant new opportunities.

What Next?

Reflect again on the definitions of hospitality shared in the first chapter of this book:

> **Hospitality** is the **attitude** and **practice** of providing the **atmosphere** and **opportunities**, however risky, in which strangers are free to become friends, thereby feeling accepted, included, and loved. The relationship thus opens up the possibility for eventual communion among the host, the stranger, and God.
>
> **Hospitality** involves recognizing the presence of Christ in family, friends, coworkers, neighbors, and complete strangers. It means responding to others as we would respond to the presence of Christ in our midst.

Relationships with the strangers in our lives become transformed when we view them through the lens of hospitality. Rather than fearing the stranger as a potential enemy, we focus on the stranger as a potential friend brought into our lives by our loving God. That potential friend may prove to be a source of blessings to our own lives and to the life of the congregation, and we may be called to provide blessings to that friend.

We encourage you to prayerfully consider what has been shared in this book and to involve others with you in study and discussion. While any one of us can practice hospitality, transforming power comes when an entire congregation grasps the vision of what it means to be a welcoming congregation. The *Study Guide* at the end of this book can enhance church-wide discussion of these concepts. We also hope you will consider reading and studying our books *Worship and Hospitality* and *Hospitality: Life in a Time of Fear.*

As you seek to increase the practice of hospitality in your own life and in the life of your congregation, remember the admonition and promise in the Letter to the Hebrews:

> **Do not neglect to show hospitality to strangers, for by doing that some have entertained angels without knowing it [13:2].**

Hospitality Checkups and Congregational Studies

Concept: Our hospitality may not always be as strong as we believe it to be. Hospitality audits, surveys, congregational studies, and interviews can help us better understand the needs and the potential of the congregation.

Seeking continuous improvement in all that an organization does and responding to the needs and desires of those being served can't happen without intentionality. In congregational life, we can identify more than one target for the services we offer and more than one factor that influences our mission and our aims:

- The church always acknowledges that faithfulness to God who has made us, to Christ who has saved us, and to the Holy Spirit, who guides and sustains us, must shape everything else that we do. Those deep theological roots set us apart from other organizations. We are not just another business or social service agency or nurturing group. The Bible and the traditions to which we belong are of great importance in the decisions we make. We practice hospitality not because it is an "effective" strategy but because our Lord wishes us to do so.

- Clearly the members of the congregation are the ones who, individually and corporately, work by God's grace to carry out the mission of the church. We are also the ones who are served by many of the programs of the church as an organization. We should all experience the hospitality of the church as we interact with one another, and we are the ones who offer hospitality to our guests.

- Outreach to persons outside the congregation should always be a substantial part of our mission. We have been given Good News to share with others, and the hospitality that runs through our lives will do much to determine the openness of others to that good news.

- Outreach also comes in service to individuals, to groups, to society, and to the world in which we have been placed. Servant evangelism, mission work, social action, and other strategies are central to the work of the church and are also means through which we show our hospitality to all people.

Thus prayer, Bible study, and true efforts at discerning our mission and our more specific aims must be a major part of decision-making in the life of the church. We must not, however, neglect the importance of receiving careful input, not only from the leaders of the congregation, but also from all the members, and we need to have sensitivity to the needs, interests, and concerns of persons outside of the church.

Hospitality Audit

Have a task force do a complete hospitality audit of your church, looking at it from the perspective of a person driving by or visiting for the first time. Include on the task force at least one person who is a relatively new member of the congregation. Use the results of the audit to identify areas for needed change, and refer those to appropriate persons and groups in the congregation. Consider matters like these:

□ Is your church easy to find? Do you need new signs on major roads or streets near the church?

□ Is your church's name easy to read from the road?

□ Is it easy to tell which entrance to use for the church office? For the sanctuary? For Sunday school or evening programs?

□ Does the exterior of your church look well-maintained and attractive?

□ Does the landscaping need attention?

□ Are there a few parking spots close to the building reserved for the disabled? For visitors? Do you have adequate parking for all who come?

□ Are the sidewalks, the entrance, and the interior spaces of the church easy to navigate for persons in wheelchairs or with other mobility concerns?

□ Are the restrooms clean? Without rust or mildew? Do you have lotion and tissues available?

□ Are all rooms in the church clearly marked? Are there clear directional signs to classrooms?

□ Do you have adequate lighting in hallways, classrooms, and the sanctuary?

□ Are there stacks of old bulletins, old magazines, or out-of-date church brochures that should be discarded?

□ Are there current, attractive handouts or brochures containing information about your church that would be helpful to visitors?

□ Are the bulletin boards current? Visitors are in fact more likely than regular members to read the bulletin boards!

□ Are there any rooms that need to be cleaned? Painted? Do some rooms look too institutional?

□ Do you have old linoleum or tile that should be replaced with carpet?

□ Are the rooms for infants and toddlers both attractive and clean? Do you have older bedding and toys that should be replaced?

□ Are extra copies of curriculum and Bibles in the classrooms? Are teachers prepared and trained to welcome visitors?

□ Are the instructions in your bulletins and worship services clear to visitors? Remember that you could have visitors who have not been to any church before coming to yours.

□ Are large print bulletins available? Is hearing amplification available?

□ Do you have mints available for persons who experience coughing or a dry throat during the service?

□ Do the announcements and/or joys and concerns time contain "insider" references that could make a visitor feel excluded? Do people identify themselves before sharing?

□ Do you have a name tag system that is current and utilized?

□ Do you have greeters positioned at the entrances to the church? Would greeters in the parking lot make it easier for your guests? Are greeters and ushers prepared to welcome guests? Do you offer training for greeters and ushers?

□ Are all members of the congregation prepared to welcome visitors? Have you provided training in hospitality?

□ Are refreshments available at a fellowship time and/or during Sunday school classes?

□ Do you have members who go out of their way during fellowship time to greet visitors and introduce them to others?

□ Are members of your church prepared to extend brunch or dinner invitations to your guests?

□ Do you have a system in place to respond to visitors within forty-eight hours of their attendance by leaving a small gift at their homes? Freshly baked cookies or bread, a devotional booklet, flowers, or a mug bearing your church's name are all possibilities.

□ Interview people who have recently visited your church and ask them for feedback. Talk to people who have continued to come—and to those who only came once.

Surveys

Congregational surveys can be one of the most helpful tools for understanding the feelings, needs, concerns, and hopes of the members of the church—and also of visitors and constituents who may complete such forms. Most surveys should be relatively short in order to obtain as high a response rate as possible.

For some special emphases, teams of people may actually visit homes to share the surveys. Most of the time, inclusion of the survey in the bulletin for two weeks in a row and in at least one issue of the newsletter will reach a sufficiently large group to provide helpful information.

The three sample surveys that follow differ considerably in complexity. The first survey is an example of one that can be used for feedback on worship services and as an aid in sermon preparation for those focusing on quality in a traditional worship service. The second survey offers a quick check-up on hospitality and outreach. The third survey is one used with congregations working on a mission statement, on substantial decisions about the future, or on solutions for a significant problem in the life of the congregation. The third survey has been used in a large number of congregations, so there is information available for meaningful comparisons between congregations. That survey also gives considerable insight into the basic beliefs and values of the congregation.

You would want to modify any of these surveys to fit the specific needs of your congregation. We share these as examples to help you in the process. You have our permission to use the form and wording of the surveys in any way you wish within your congregation.

Worship Survey

As the Worship Commission, the pastors, the music director, and the choirs make plans for worship in the weeks and months ahead, it would be helpful to us to know how you feel about our worship services. Any suggestions you have would be very much appreciated. You do not have to put your name on this survey. Use the reverse side if you need more space for comments.

Which service do you normally attend? (check one)
___ 9 A.M.   ___ 10:30 A.M.   ___ Both

Rate each of the following on a scale from 1 to 5, with 1 being "not at all satisfied" and 5 being "very satisfied." 2, 3, and 4 represent intermediate positions:
___ The quality of the worship service as a whole.
___ The quality of the sermons.
___ The quality of the choral music.
___ The quality of congregational hymns.
___ The quality of the children's sermons.
___ The quality of our welcome to visitors.

We began using name tags for all members six months ago. Check as many of these responses as reflect your opinion:
___ I have learned the names of some people that I did not know because of the name tags.
___ I find myself starting some conversations that I might not have begun before we had the name tags.
___ I wear my name tag every Sunday.
___ I frequently forget to wear my name tag.
___ Overall, I feel good about the use of name tags.
___ Overall, I wish we would stop using name tags.

What suggestions, if any, do you have for the pastors in terms of themes, topics, or biblical emphases to be covered in sermons?

What suggestions, if any, do you have for hymns you would especially like to sing?

What other suggestions, if any, do you have for improving our worship services?

Hospitality and Outreach Survey

Please do not put your name on this survey. We want people to share their honest opinions, and that is sometimes a more comfortable task when names are not placed on the form. We do need some information about you to help in evaluating overall survey results:

1. Which of the following best describes your relationship to this congregation? Check one:
   ___ Member
   ___ Constituent (frequent in attendance but not a formal member)
   ___ Preparatory member (intend to join the church but am not yet old enough or need to complete membership classes)
   ___ Visitor
2. If you are a member of this congregation, for how many years have you belonged? (Leave blank if not a member) _____

Use these symbols to express the strength of your agreement or disagreement with the statements that follow:

SA	=	*Strongly Agree*
A	=	*Agree*
D	=	*Disagree*
SD	=	*Strongly Disagree*
NO	=	*No Opinion*

____ 3. A Christian has an obligation to share his or her faith with others.

____ 4. I have experienced opportunities to share my faith with others.

____ 5. I actively seek opportunities to invite others to come to our church.

____ 6. I can think of at least five people who do not attend any church on a regular basis with whom I have a friendly relationship.

____ 7. Seeking to build relationships with people who are outside the church is one of my priorities.

____ 8. In our congregation, people go out of their way to be friendly to strangers and newcomers.

____ 9. A single parent can find welcome and acceptance in our congregation.

____ 10. A person who is struggling with a problem such as alcoholism or other drug addiction can find welcome and acceptance in our congregation.

____ 11. In our congregation, people care for one another in a way that is more compassionate than what I have experienced in other groups.

(over)

168

_____ 12. In our congregation, there are cliques or exclusive groups that make one feel unwelcome.

_____ 13. Our congregation makes a conscious effort to get new people involved in a Sunday school class, Bible study, or spiritual growth group.

_____ 14. At church, I take the initiative to talk with those I do not know well.

_____ 15. Our church respects diversity of opinion and does not put people down for expressing disagreement.

_____ 16. I'd have to say that I don't feel accepted in this congregation.

_____ 17. It is important for this church to reach out to persons who are not members.

_____ 18. Building the quality of the spiritual lives of people in the church is more important than seeing the church grow in numbers.

_____ 19. Our pastors should spend as much time in ministry to unchurched people as to people in our church.

_____ 20. In our congregation, we really see meeting the needs of our own members as our major concern.

_____ 21. Our congregation makes a conscious effort to give new members meaningful roles or tasks based on their spiritual gifts and interests.

_____ 22. I am open to new experiences and ideas.

_____ 23. People in our congregation are open to new experiences and ideas.

_____ 24. I think being a part of the church means being a part of the church's ministry—care of members and outreach to the world are part of what it means to be a disciple.

25. Please add any comments that you would like about our congregation's efforts to reach out to others in the name of Christ and about the hospitality that people encounter when they are guests at worship and other church activities.

Congregational Survey

The instructions and the survey that follow origin-
ally were printed on 8 1/2" X 11" paper and have
been reduced to fit the pages in this book.

One of the most valuable tools in developing a profile of your church is the use of a congregational survey. The one that follows has been developed with care and used in a wide range of settings. Christian Community has data on file which makes it possible to compare the results from your church with those of other churches.

You may decide that you want to add some questions to the survey, based on particular issues and needs in your church. You should certainly feel free to do so and also to modify the visual appearance of the questionnaire (to put it, for example, on a paper size that comfortably fits in a Sunday morning bulletin or newsletter).

You need to determine the best, most realistic means to distribute the survey in your congregation. Some approaches used by other churches include:

- Putting the survey in the bulletin on two consecutive Sunday mornings, with the request that each mem-ber of the congregation only complete the survey one time. Some churches have actually provided time during the worship service for people to complete the questionnaire. That may or may not be appropriate and comfortable in your setting.

- Mailing the survey to every member of the congre-gation and also to those persons who have been recent visitors. Those who have put stamps on a return envelope have had the highest percentage of returns.

- Using the survey as a part of cottage meetings (meetings in the homes of members) and having discussions about the survey after members have had time to complete them.

- Employing a combination of the above means to

obtain the maximum possible response rate from the church.

You want as many persons as possible to complete the survey. Teenagers should certainly be encouraged to complete surveys themselves, and some churches have asked children as young as ten years of age to complete surveys. You also want to include constituents of your church; constituents are those persons who are not formal members but who attend frequently and often function in many ways as though they were members. Also consider asking some persons who are visitors to your congregation to complete the survey; data from visitors can be very interesting when compared to that from those who are already members.

Congregational Survey

Please do not put your name on this survey. We want people to share their honest opinions, and that is sometimes a more comfortable task when names are not placed on the form. We do need some information about you to help in evaluating overall survey results:

1. Which of the following best describes your relationship to this congregation? Check one:
    ___ Member
    ___ Constituent (frequent in attendance but not a formal member)
    ___ Preparatory member (intend to join the church but am not yet old enough or need to complete membership classes)
    ___ Visitor

2. If you are a member of this congregation, for how many years have you belonged? (Leave blank if not a member) _____

3. Check one: ___ Male ___ Female

4. Check one: ___ Married ___ Single (never married)
    ___ Divorced ___ Widow or widower

5. Check one to indicate your age range:
    ___ 65 or older ___ 18–26
    ___ 51–64 ___ 12–17
    ___ 36–50 ___ 11 or under
    ___ 27–35

Use these symbols to indicate how often you personally do each of the following:

D   =   *Daily*
W   =   *Weekly*
MM =   *More than once a month (not weekly or daily)*
OM =   *Once a month*
LM =   *Less than once a month*
N   =   *Never*

_____ 6. Attend worship services.

_____ 7. Attend Sunday School or another regular class or study group.

_____ 8. Participate in church activities other than worship or Sunday School.

_____ 9. Get together socially with people who are members of the church.

_____ 10. Volunteer time to help the church's program (teach, serve on a committee,....).

_____ 11. Volunteer time to help the church's outreach to nonmembers (visit in homes, make phone calls, write notes,....).

_____ 12. Volunteer time to help the church's outreach to persons in need (food pantry, tutoring,....).

_____ 13. Volunteer time in community activities that are not part of the church.

Use these symbols to express the strength of your agreement or disagreement with the statements which follow:

SA	=	*Strongly Agree*
A	=	*Agree*
D	=	*Disagree*
SD	=	*Strongly Disagree*
NO	=	*No Opinion*

_____ 14. My religious faith is the main factor in all my decision-making.

_____ 15. My experiences at church help me grow closer to God.

_____ 16. My experiences at church help me in my daily life.

_____ 17. My faith in God is stronger now than it was five years ago.

_____ 18. My faith in God affects my decisions more now than five years ago.

_____ 19. The Bible is the actual Word of God and is to be taken literally.

_____ 20. The Bible is divinely inspired and its basic moral teachings are true, even though it may contain some human error.

_____ 21. Studying the Bible helps me in my daily life.

_____ 22. I believe Jesus Christ is the divine Son of God.

_____ 23. People who do not believe in Christ will not go to heaven.

_____ 24. I believe in life after death.

_____ 25. I can think of specific times when God has answered my prayers.

_____ 26. Personal success is a sign of God's blessings.

_____ 27. A person is "saved" or put right with God based on how good a life that person has lived.

_____ 28. A person is "saved" or put right with God not because of works but because of God's grace.

_____ 29. A Christian has an obligation to share his or her faith with others.

_____ 30. It is important for this church to reach out to persons who are not members.

_____ 31. A Christian has an obligation to work for peace.

_____ 32. It is important for this church to work for peace.

_____ 33. A Christian has an obligation to care for those who have physical needs (for food, housing, medical care,....).

_____ 34. It is important for this church to care for those who have physical needs (for food, housing, medical care,....).

_____ 35. Our worship services meet my needs and help improve my spiritual life.

_____ 36.   Overall the Sunday School or Christian education program at the church does a good job meeting my needs.

_____ 37.   Members are well-informed about what the boards, committees, and other church organizations are doing.

_____ 38.   Every member of the church who is capable and interested has an equal chance to hold a key leadership position.

_____ 39.   Disagreements and conflicts in the church are dealt with openly and fairly rather than hidden behind closed doors.

_____ 40.   The current morale of members of this church is very high.

_____ 41.   I am excited about what will happen in the future of this church.

_____ 42.   Members of this church are similar in values and lifestyle to people who live immediately around the church.

_____ 43.   Our church is very involved with the community around the church.

_____ 44.   In our congregation, people go out of their way to be friendly to strangers and newcomers.

_____ 45.   A single parent can find welcome and acceptance in our congregation.

_____ 46.   A person who is struggling with a problem such as alcoholism or other drug addiction can find welcome and acceptance in our congregation.

_____ 47.   In our congregation, people care for one another in a way that is more compassionate than what I have experienced in other groups.

_____ 48.   In our congregation, there are cliques or exclusive groups which make one feel unwelcome.

_____ 49.   Our congregation makes a conscious effort to get new people involved in a Sunday school class, Bible study, or spiritual growth group.

_____ 50.   At church, I take the initiative to talk with those I do not know well.

_____ 51.   Our church respects diversity of opinion and does not put people down for expressing disagreement.

_____ 52.   I'd have to say that I don't feel accepted in this congregation.

_____ 53.   It's easy for a new member of this church to become involved in leadership positions.

_____ 54.   This church makes decisions mainly by formal organizational procedures.

_____ 55.   This church makes decisions mainly by informal conversations.

_____ 56.   Our congregation strongly affirms and expresses our denominational heritage.

_____ 57.   I want the minister of the church to take initiative in starting needed programs and improvements for the church.

_____ 58. I want the minister of the church to help implement the programs and ideas of members.

_____ 59. In my opinion, our church is too dependent on the minister (and any other employed staff) for leadership.

_____ 60. In my opinion, our church doesn't do enough to encourage the minister (and any other employed staff) to show leadership.

_____ 61. I believe a Christian should be involved in working for social justice (racial issues, drug problems,...).

_____ 62. I believe the church should be involved in working for social justice (racial issues, drug problems,...).

_____ 63. I believe our church does a good job working for social justice (racial issues, drug problems,...).

As you think about the future of our church, which of the following should receive more emphasis, less emphasis, or the same emphasis as at the present time? Use these symbols for your response:

ME = More Emphasis
SE = Same Emphasis
LE = Less Emphasis

_____ 64. Providing quality worship services.

_____ 65. Providing quality Sunday School and Christian education.

_____ 66. Providing quality youth programs.

_____ 67. Providing quality young adult (18–35) programs.

_____ 68. Providing quality mid-life (36–64) programs.

_____ 69. Providing quality senior citizen programs.

_____ 70. Reaching out to nonmembers and helping the church grow.

_____ 71. Helping meet the physical needs of people.

_____ 72. Working for world peace.

_____ 73. Working for social justice.

_____ 74. Providing quality pastoral care for our members.

_____ 75. Increasing our understanding of denominational heritage.

_____ 76. Deepening the spiritual life of members.

_____ 77. Other: _____

_____ 78. Other: _____

Interviews

Interviews provide another helpful way to gain information about how members and potential members feel about the congregation's ministry. Interviews have three obvious disadvantages over written surveys:

- They are a much more time-consuming way to get information.

- It can be more difficult to collate (gather together) information when several different persons are doing the interviewing.

- People will sometimes hold back on what they really feel out of respect for the feelings of the person doing the interviewing.

On the other hand, interviews offer some distinct advantages:

- Instead of simply wondering what a person means by a written comment, it's possible for the interviewer to ask for clarification.

- Most people will share more suggestions in response to an interview than in response to a written survey.

- Although the process takes longer, it's generally possible to obtain a higher response rate with interviews than with written surveys. Although scheduling a convenient time may be difficult, most people will agree to an interview.

- The interview, if properly done, provides a positive point of contact between the person interviewed and the church in a way that is not normally possible with a written survey.

Because of the amount of time consumed by an interview, it's generally best to think of these as ways to gain information in specific areas rather than as a strategy for gaining input from each person in the congregation. There may occasionally be issues significant enough (such as a potential move to a new location) to justify an interview with every member of the church.

Here are some examples of specific groups of people in situations in which interviews can be helpful:

- The last ten persons who joined your congregation to discover why they joined, how well-integrated they currently feel, and what suggestions they would have to offer the church in its efforts to reach new members.

- The last ten persons who left your congregation for reasons other than a move to another geographical location to discover why they left and what suggestions they would have to offer the church in its efforts to retain members.

- The last ten persons who visited the congregation to discover why they came, how they felt about the worship service (or whatever event or group they attended), how they felt about their welcome by the congregation, and whether or not they intend to continue attending.

- The parents of youth group members to discover how they feel about the youth program and what concerns they have about their young people with which the church might be able to help.

- The young adults in the congregation to discover how they feel about the church and what suggestions they have for improving outreach to persons in their age bracket.

- The members of the congregation who live in nursing homes or who are shut-ins to discover what the church can do to help improve the quality of their lives.

- Those who have been chairpersons of committees and boards for the past year to learn how they felt about their work in the church and what would have increased their pleasure in that work.

Interviews can be conducted on the basis of written survey items, with the person doing the interviewing checking off the appropriate responses. They can also be based on questions which are considerably more open-ended, such as the following, for persons who have joined the congregation in the last twelve months:

- What caused you to visit our congregation the first time?

- Why did you come back after your first visit?

- Why did you join our congregation?

- What things has the church done that have helped you feel welcome?

- What things, if any, has the church done that have caused you to feel less than 100% welcomed and appreciated?

- What opportunities do you want in the future from our congregation (classes, programs, services, etc.)?

- What suggestions would you offer our congregation for doing a more effective job reaching out to those who are unchurched?

We'd Like to Hear from You

We hope that the strategies which we've suggested in this chapter and in this book will help bring about greater hospitality and other needed changes in the life of your church. We would love to hear about your experiences with hospitality. You can contact us through regular mail or through e-mail:

Fred Bernhard and Steve Clapp
Christian Community and LifeQuest
6404 S. Calhoun Street
Fort Wayne, Indiana 46807
DadofTia@aol.com

Resources and References

This list includes publications to which reference was made in the book and other resources of which we want you to be aware. Those marked with an asterisk (*) are available through Christian Community/LifeQuest (800–774–3360) or Brethren Press (800–323–8039).

A **Study Guide** to accompany **Widening the Welcome of Your Church** is included at the end of this edition. The guide provides help for those who want to use **Widening the Welcome of Your Church** for small group, Sunday school class, administrative group, or retreat study.

Barna, George, *User Friendly Churches*. Ventura: Regal Books, 1991. Based on careful research, an excellent look at changing the climate in the church.

Benson, Peter, *The Troubled Journey*. Minneapolis: Search Institute, 1990, 1993. Results of a massive and also comprehensive study of youth in the United States. Filled with useful information on understanding youth culture and identifying areas where the church should consider new programming. Search's resources are all excellent for people working with youth. Write for a catalog: Search Institute, Thresher Square West, Suite 210, 700 South Third Street, Minneapolis, MN 55415.

Boling, Ruth, *A Children's Guide to Worship*. Geneva Press, 2000. Helping children feel comfortable in worship.

*Bontrager Ed, *Building a Multicultural Congregation*. Fort Wayne: LifeQuest and New Life Ministries, 2003. A practical book with strategies for "widening the welcome of your church" to other cultures. This book talks about ways to develop inclusive worship, find the right leader-ship, share facilities with ethnic congregations, and begin a church of another ethnic group. This comes in a convenient notebook form with permission to photocopy.

Campolo, Tony and Gordon Aeschliman, *Fifty Ways You Can Share Your Faith.* Downers Grove: InterVarsity Press 1992. Extremely practical ways you can reach out with Christ's love in actions as well as words.

A Church for the 21st Century. Indianapolis: Center for Congregational Growth and Vitality (Division of Homeland Ministries, The Christian Church). This outstanding video will help churches of any denomination begin dealing with the changes needed for effective outreach.

*Clapp, Steve and Fred Bernhard, *Hospitality: Life in a Time of Fear.* Fort Wayne: LifeQuest. This book deals directly with the tough questions raised by the tragic events of September 11, 2001, and reveals that the answer to fear is not turning inward but turning outward. Learning to recognize the presence of Christ in others can have a liberating impact on all that we do and can enable us to move past the fears that threaten to immobilize us. This is an excellent guide to the development of hospitality as a part of the spiritual life and shows how hospitality relates to our faith, our homes, our neighborhoods, our places of work, and even our driving. Includes discussion questions for classes and small groups.

*Clapp, Steve and Fred Bernhard, *Worship and Hospitality.* Fort Wayne: LifeQuest. Looks at worship through the lens of hospitality. This book is an effort to move beyond the tension among traditional, contemporary, and blended worship to create worship which speaks to the deepest needs of people and builds up the church as the body of Christ. A guide for individual or group study is included.

*Clapp, Steve and Kristen Leverton, *Fifty Strategies for Outreach to Teenagers.* Elgin: The Andrew Center, 1996. Creative, practical strategies to reach teenagers who have become inactive in the church or who have never been involved in the church.

*Clapp, Steve, *One Hundred Ways to Reach Young Singles, Couples, and Families.* Fort Wayne: LifeQuest, 2004. Practical ideas that have been tested in churches around the country. This is an excellent starting place if your church needs to expand its outreach to young adults.

*Clapp, Steve, *Overcoming Barriers to Church Growth*. Elgin: The Andrew Center, 1994. If you can't get people in your church interested in evangelism, get this book! It includes a very helpful section on low self-esteem in individuals, congregations, and denominations as a sometimes overlooked barrier to church growth. A new edition will come in 2005 or 2006.

*Clapp, Steve and Sam Detwiler, *Peer Evangelism*. Elgin: Brethren Press, 1993. Faith-sharing for teenagers. Designed for use in Sunday school classes, youth groups, or retreats.

*Clapp, Steve and Sam Detwiler, *Sharing Living Water*. Fort Wayne: LifeQuest, 1996, 2000, 2001. This book is an excellent companion to the one you are holding in your hands! While most church members readily agree that they should share their faith with others and invite them to church, many are not comfortable doing so. This practical, easy-to-understand book helps people identify the natural connecting points that give opportunities to share their faith or invite others to church without being manipulative or feeling awkward. The book discusses both verbal and nonverbal ways to share one's faith.

*Clapp, Steve, Kristen Leverton Helbert, and Angela Zizak, *Faith Matters: Teenagers, Sexuality, and Religion*. Fort Wayne: LifeQuest, 2003. Results of a comprehensive study of almost six thousand church-active teens, which looked at the relationship between their religious faith and their sexual behavior and values. The results of this study were released at a congressional briefing in Washington, D.C. Contains many practical suggestions for churches that want to improve their hospitality to young people and help them with decisions related to dating, marriage, and sexuality.

Delatte, Paul, *Commentary on the Rule of St. Benedict*. London: Burns and Oates, 1921. A classic work for those interested in this order and the practice of hospitality.

*Detwiler, Sam and Steve Clapp, *The Church of Recovery*. Fort Wayne: LifeQuest, 2002. Strategies for extending the hospitality of the church to persons who have problems with addiction. Recognizing the usefulness of the 12-step approach as a means of deepening the spiritual life for all people.

Easum, William M., *Sacred Cows Make Gourmet Burgers*. Nashville: Abingdon, 1995. Fasten your seat belts, because this book will turn your thinking about the church upside down—and it will disturb you because Easum is right!

Emerging Trends. A publication of the Princeton Religion Research Center (47 Hulfish Street, Suite 215, P.O. Box 389, Princeton, New Jersey 08542). Has excellent reports on the relationship between religious faith and secular culture. Subscriptions are somewhat expensive, but this newsletter has information you won't find elsewhere.

Frounfelker, Grace Moyer, *As a Little Child*. Scottdale: Herald Press, 1998. A great book on helping children feel welcome in the life of the church.

Gibble, Kenneth L., "Diversity: A Gift Sometimes Difficult to Receive," *The Messenger*, Vol. 144, No. 10, November, 1995, pp. 20–21. An exceptionally well written article, especially interesting for Anabaptists.

Hall, Eddy and Gary Morsch, *The Lay Ministry Revolution*. Grand Rapids: Baker, 1995. An outstanding book on empowering lay people for ministry and setting them free to do it.

*Helbert, Kristen Leverton and Dick Benner, *Public Relations Kit: Help from a Hospitality Perspective*. Fort Wayne: LifeQuest and New Life Ministries, 2003. Media exposure and publicity can play a valuable role not only in a church's evangelistic efforts but also in its outreach ministries. This practical kit, which comes with permission to photocopy, shares how the Internet, newspapers, radio, television, direct mail, the yellow pages, the telephone, the appearance of the church, and the attitudes of people can all contribute to the church as a place of hospitality.

*Hershey, S. Joan with foreword by Steve Clapp, *The First Thirty Seconds: A Guide to Hospitality for Greeters and Ushers*. Fort Wayne: LifeQuest and New Life Ministries, 1999,

2002, 2004. Greeters and ushers are the "first contact" with the congregation for many who visit. The number one question visitors want answered is: "Is this a friendly congregation?" This booklet offers clear training for greeters and ushers, with an emphasis on hospitality. Giving copies to all greeters and ushers in your church can help widen your church's welcome.

*Hershey, S. Joan and Steve Clapp, *Healthy Pastor–Healthy Church!* Fort Wayne: LifeQuest, 2003. Practical suggestions for improving the health and the effectiveness of pastors. Hospitality in the congregation should extend to the way in which pastors and their families are treated.

*Hershey, S. Joan, *Invite a Friend Kit.* Fort Wayne: LifeQuest and New Life Ministries, 2004. This kit will provide you with a thorough step-by-step action plan for an "Invite a Friend Sunday." The kit includes five copies of the new booklet *A Guide to an Effective Invite a Friend Sunday* as well as a timeline for planning the event, ideas for engaging congregational participation, and sample printed resources.

History of the Church of the Brethren—Eastern Pennsylvania, edited by S.R. Zug, New Era Printing: Lancaster, 1915. A very helpful reference for this book; primarily of interest to those studying Anabaptist history.

Keifert, Patrick, *Welcoming the Stranger.* Minneapolis: Fortress Press, 1992. This is an excellent overview of hospitality with special attention given to issues related to worship.

Kew, Richard and Roger J. White, *New Millennium, New Church.* Boston: Cowley Publications, 1992. (Cowley Publications, 28 Temple Place, Boston, Massachusetts 02111) Especially written from the Episcopal perspective but applicable to most mainline congregations and denominations. Very helpful in understanding the dynamics at work in most mainline churches today.

Kramp, John, *Out of Their Faces and into Their Shoes.* Nashville: Broadman and Holman Publishing, 1995. This is the best contemporary book on faith-sharing we've seen except the one written by Steve Clapp and Sam Detwiler!

Mead, Loren, *Transforming Congregations for the Future*. Bethesda: The Alban Institute, 1994. An insightful book— helping congregations move into the future. Emphasizes spiritual transformation and institutional change.

Meagher, Robert E., "Stranger at the Gate," in *Parabola 2*, No. 4 (1977), pp. 10–15. This was very helpful in preparation of this book; will be of interest primarily to those seeking more historical background and perspective.

Miller, Donald L., "Brethren and Church Growth," in *Brethren Life and Thought*, Winter, 1980. This is the original essay that got the Oakland Church and Fred Bernhard excited about hospitality! Miller is an excellent scholar and communicator.

Miller, Herb, *Connecting with God*. Nashville: Abingdon, 1994. This is a wonderful book on nurturing the spiritual life of the congregation. You should have a copy.

Miller, Keith, *A Hunger for Healing*. San Francisco: HarperSanFrancisco, 1991. This ground-breaking book shows how the 12-step model relates to the classic spiritual disciplines and can be used to deepen the spiritual life. This book also communicates a great deal about authentic hospitality and caring.

*Mundey, Paul, *Unlocking Church Doors: 10 Keys to Positive Change*. Nashville: Abingdon, 1999. While change is not the only factor that contributes to the vitality of a congregation, resistance to change can prevent a church from accomplishing its mission. Mundey provides a toolbox of ideas to help leaders transform their congregations.

Net Results. (Cokesbury Subscription Services, 201 Eighth Ave., S, Nashville, TN 37202) A monthly publication published in cooperation with the evangelism departments of several major denominations. New ideas for evangelism, church vitality, and leadership in each issue. A subscription to this is one of the best investments you can make.

Peck, M. Scott, *Further Along the Road Less Traveled*. New York: Simon and Schuster, 1993. A book that has changed lives! Very helpful in understanding ourselves and others.

Peck, M. Scott and Marilyn Von Walder, *Gifts for the Journey.* San Francisco: HarperSanFrancisco, 1985, 1995. Many people seem unaware of this beautiful book on the Christian faith. Also available with an audio tape.

Posterski, Donald C., *Reinventing Evangelism.* Downers Grove: InterVarsity Press, 1989. A thought-provoking book which truly speaks to both the Canadian and the U.S. church.

Schaller, Lyle E., *Strategies for Change.* Nashville: Abingdon, 1993. If your church is struggling with change *or* if it needs to be struggling with change, this book will help!

Schaller, Lyle E., *The Very Large Church.* Nashville: Abingdon Press, 2000. Looks at the different issues involved in giving leadership to a large congregation including issues of relationships and hospitality.

Study Guide:

Widening the Welcome of Your Church

By Steve Clapp

Suggestions for Using This Study Guide

1. This study is suggested for use in adult Sunday School classes, Bible study groups, church boards, church committees, mission groups, or staff groups focusing on the improving the hospitality of the congregation. This *Guide* may also be used for individual study, but most suggestions are group-oriented.

2. Some sessions may offer more activities than time permits. Extra suggestions may be carried over to the next session, or you may choose those most suitable for your group's interests, needs, and size.

3. The *Guide* is designed for as many as thirteen sessions but may be used for smaller numbers of sessions. Choose the combination of topics most beneficial to your group, but be sure to include sessions 1, 2, 3, and 6 in any study. In some instances, you may want to scan the intervening material and share a short summary of it where needed to maintain continuity.

4. Remember that every group has both active and passive learners. Try to involve participants in a variety of ways, remaining sensitive to personalities and preferences. Encourage, but do not force, participation. Allow "I pass" as an acceptable response.

5. Having class members use different translations of the Bible will enrich your discussions and give new perspective.

6. Your leadership will be easier if you read the designated chapter in *Widening the Welcome of Your Church* and the accompanying session outline in this *Guide* before the time of the class or group meeting. There are also some sessions for which you may want to photocopy one or more pages from the book *Widening the Welcome of Your Church* so that group members do not have to write in their books. The session plans assume that you will photocopy the indicated materials and that a chalkboard or some newsprint is available each week. Other needed preparation will either be indicated near the start of the session plan or will be listed under "Optional Preparation."

Session One:
Hospitality: Not Optional and Not Safe

Widening the Welcome of Your Church **Reference:** This is an initial session, so it is possible that group participants may not yet have received copies of the book. This session focuses on the first chapter, *Hospitality: Not Optional and Not Safe* (pages 13–23), in such a way that group members do not have to have read it in advance.

Biblical Focus: Romans 15:7–13 (on welcoming one another and recognizing that the Gospel is for all people).

Optional Preparation: Put together a short video clip of news stories about threats to personal safety such as burglaries, car jackings, and pick-pockets; simply recording a few minutes of the evening news is generally sufficient, though some may prefer to develop a more sophisticated selection from several television programs. OR—Have available a selection of recent newspapers and news magazines which group members can search for headlines.

Opening:
1. Focus the group's attention on the fears that we experience in today's society. Use one of these approaches, depending on whether the optional preparation has been done:
- Show a short video clip of various threats to personal safety.
- Have group members turn through newspapers and news magazines to identify headlines about things which cause us fear and anxiety, such as burglaries, murders, drug deals, fires, and accidents from drunken drivers.
- Have group members brainstorm various threats to personal safety which we experience today. Write those on a chalkboard or newsprint.

2. Then ask:
- How do such threats to safety affect our attitudes toward strangers?
- Do you feel as though you are personally accustomed to immediately welcoming people you do not know, or are you more likely to wait and see how people seem to respond to you? Why?

Looking into the Scripture:
3. Read or have a volunteer read **Romans 15:7–13**. Point out that the ministry of Jesus to the Jewish people confirmed what the patriarchs had been promised, but the salvation Jesus offers is for the Gentiles as well. Paul makes the openness to

Study Guide – Page 189

Gentiles clear by quoting Psalm 18:49, Deuteronomy 32:43, Psalm 117:1, and Isaiah 11:10. Discuss:
- Does Jesus put any restrictions on the welcome we are asked to give in Romans 15:7? Why, or why not?
- What does the fact that Jesus speaks so much about the message being for Gentiles as well as Jews say about the openness we should have in our congregations toward those who are "outsiders?"

Looking into *Widening the Welcome of Your Church*:
4. Summarize or read the childhood experiences of Fred or of Steve (pages 14–16). Invite group members to share some of their childhood experiences with strangers. Discuss: In what ways is life different today than when you were a child as far as welcoming strangers is concerned? In what ways does it remain the same? What price do we pay when we live in constant fear of strangers? In what ways does news coverage sometimes make the world seem more dangerous than it may actually be?

5. Summarize or read the church visiting experiences of Fred or of Steve (pages 18–19), OR share a similar experience you've had. How do you feel about the statement of the authors that: "To have such things happen is an abomination to the Christ we serve"? Why do we sometimes fail to be as welcoming as we should be? Why do many of us need to make a special effort in order to be more welcoming?

Closing:
6. Have group members look at the definition of hospitality that appears in the box on page 22. Share some of the background about that statement provided on pages 21–23. Be sure to note that there are dangers to hospitality—"And possibly the most distinct and frightening danger of all is that practicing hospitality may change our lives." Close with a time of prayer, seeking God's guidance as a group and as a congregation in learning to widen the welcome of the church to all people.

Challenge: Observe the interactions between members and visitors before and after worship services. How do people in our congregation respond to visitors? How do they respond to us? What initial changes do you see that need to be made?

Session Two:
A Biblical Look at Hospitality

Widening the Welcome of Your Church **Reference:** *A Biblical Look at Hospitality* (pages 25–32). Surprise people with snacks as they enter the room. You might offer cookies and hot chocolate or coffee; a fruit and cheese tray; or a variety of chips and dips. You may wish to recruit one or two volunteers to help provide the snacks, but the activity will work best if most group members do not know there will be refreshments.
Biblical Focus: Genesis 18:1–15 (the hospitality of Abraham and Sarah to three strangers). **Matthew 25:31–46** (on helping "the least of these" being the same as giving service to Christ).

Opening:
1. Have people begin sharing in snacks as they arrive for the session. Then discuss:
   • Were you surprised when you found refreshments available? Why, or why not?
   • In what ways does sharing food make it easier to share informal conversation with others? How do you feel when another person invites you to eat a meal in his or her home or go out for breakfast, lunch, or dinner?
   • Suppose that you were seeking a new church home and visited two congregations. People in the first congregation greeted you warmly enough, but you did not hear anything more from that church during the week. People in the second congregation greeted you warmly, and two different persons asked you to share in meals that day or during the week. Which congregation would feel most welcoming? Why? For what reasons might a person turn down an invitation for a meal but still feel appreciative of that invitation?

Looking into the Scripture:
2. Point out the common components of hospitality as shared on page 26 of *Widening the Welcome of Your Church*. Explain that these components were familiar ones throughout the area we call the Ancient Near East.

3. Have **Genesis 18:1–15** read aloud with persons taking the following roles: narrator, Abraham, Sarah, and the stranger who is identified as the Lord. Discuss:
   • How does the Ancient Near East tradition of not even asking initially for the names of guests contrast with our attitude toward strangers today?
   • How would such a welcome have felt if you had been
Study Guide – Page 191

traveling in that place and time?
- What would be some comparable ways in which we can show hospitality today?

Looking into *Widening the Welcome of Your Church:*
4. Lift up some of the other information about hospitality in the Scripture which is shared in *A Biblical Look at Hospitality*.

5. Focus on the overview of biblical hospitality shared on page 32. You may wish to summarize the seven points on a chalkboard or some newsprint. Discuss:
- What difference does it make that hospitality is not simply a program in our congregation but "the very fabric of the Hebrew and Christian people"?
- Have group members share examples of persons who were once strangers who became good friends or strong positive influences. How does opening ourselves to strangers also open us to the blessings of God?

Closing:
6. Close by summarizing or having read **Matthew 25:31–46**. Ask: How would our lives be transformed if we took this passage seriously? How does it change your view of both neighbor and stranger to think of Christ being truly present in those persons? Share in the Lord's prayer to end the session.

Challenge: Think of one person from your church, your neighborhood, or your workplace whom you barely know. Focus on this person in prayer, and find a way to reach out with hospitality to that person during the week.

Session Three:
The Oakland Experience

Widening the Welcome of Your Church **Reference:** *The Oakland Experience* (pages 33–40). Recruit volunteers in advance for the opening skit, or think about which persons to draft as they enter the room. You'll want to write the starting lines of the skit on notecards for the two participants or photocopy this page for them. Make copies for group members of "Elements of Hospitality in the Church," which follows this session plan.
Biblical Focus: John 13:1–20 (Jesus washing the feet of the disciples).

Opening:

1. Begin with a skit which parodies the kind of approach to evangelism which makes most people feel uncomfortable. The initial lines are given, but the participants may wish to continue or improvise using their own creativity.

Evangelist, knocking on the door:	I sure hope they're home tonight. This is the third night in a row I've tried.
Victim, answering the door:	Can I help you?
Evangelist:	I just live a few blocks away and wanted to visit with you for a few minutes.
Victim:	What's this about? My family and I are right in the middle of supper.
Evangelist:	Well, it's about your eternal salvation, so I'd say it's pretty important.
Victim:	We already belong to St. Mark's Church, so I don't think we're interested.
Evangelist:	I didn't know you already belonged to a church. Does that really mean you don't care about salvation?
Victim:	It means my supper is getting cold.
Evangelist:	. . . . .
Victim:	. . . . .

Discuss:
- Why do the words "evangelist" and "victim" seem appropriate for this kind of interaction?
- Why do most of us feel uncomfortable with this kind of interaction? In what ways may that style of evangelism have negative rather than positive impact?

Study Guide – Page 193

2. Share some of the background information about the Oakland congregation from pages 32–33. Have group members briefly respond to how they feel about the reservations on evangelism which people in the Oakland had:
- Not feeling comfortable asking people if they are "saved."
- Anxiety about making cold calls like the one in the skit.
- Inability to feel good about oversimplifying the faith.
- The fear of rejection.

Looking into the Scripture:
3. Read aloud or have group members silently read **John 13:1–20**. Discuss:
Why was it difficult for people to accept Jesus washing their feet? What does the action of Christ suggest about the way in which we should approach other persons? Does Christ try to motivate the disciples by fear or by love? Why?

Looking into *Widening the Welcome of Your Church*:
4. Ask group members to identify one or more images of your church which they and/or others may have. For example, is it a country church, a farmers' church, a teachers' church, a white-collar church, a blue-collar church, an affluent church, a church of social climbers, a bankers' church? How widespread are those images? Are the images seen as primarily positive or negative?

5. Share copies of "Elements of Hospitality in the Church." Note that the words in italics refer to the experiences of the Oakland congregation. The question that follows each Oakland statement is one to answer for your congregation. Have people work in groups of three to five to go through the list. Talk about the questions, and check those items that appear to be areas where your church needs to do more work. Have the smaller groups report back to the total group.

Closing:
6. Go around the group, inviting each person to share thanks for one aspect of the life of your congregation. Then join together in a closing prayer.

Challenge: Visit in person or by phone with two other members of the church this week, ideally persons who are not in your study group. Ask them to share with you some of the things they appreciate about your congregation. Write those and your own appreciative thoughts on a sheet of paper that you can post in your home where you will see it often.

Elements of Hospitality in the Church

The words in italics refer to the experiences of the Oakland congregation. The question which follows each Oakland statement is one to answer for your congregation.

___ *We have emphasized that we are practicing biblical hospitality, and the Bible has been the starting place for our self-understanding and study.* Are our members clear that welcoming people is at the core of a biblical faith and not just a pragmatic strategy for church growth?

___ *We've taken training seriously. We offer classes or groups to train new people in the practice of hospitality.* Have we done enough to train members in how to be genuinely welcoming?

___ *We give people assignments to practice different aspects of hospitality.* Have we helped people move beyond theory to practice in our efforts at hospitality and growth?

___ *We began at a relatively early stage in our emphasis on hospitality to see signs of the concept affecting congregational life. We began to see people lingering more after services.* Do we see signs that our members care about visitors and truly want them to feel welcome?

___ *We had people prepared to invite visitors to their homes for lunch.* Are several of our active members prepared to take visitors home or to a restaurant for lunch?

___ *We cultivated the art of listening as a part of the practice of hospitality.* Do we really care about the needs of visitors and want to help them become integrated into the church?

___ *Classes and groups in the church began systematic strategies to reach out to those who had become inactive and to those who were potential members.* Do our classes and groups do anything to reach out to people who have stopped coming or who might start coming?

___ *In all areas of congregational life, we saw people interacting with one another in more accepting and caring ways.* Do our members show the level of care for one another which reflects deep hospitality?

___ *And yes, we certainly did experience numerical growth.* Are we experiencing numerical growth?

Session Four:
What Motivates Us?

Widening the Welcome of Your Church **Reference:** *What Motivates Us* (pages 41–50).
Biblical Focus: Luke 19:1–10 (the hospitality of Zacchaeus the tax collector to Jesus).
Optional Preparation: Have recent visitors to your church meet with your group to share their impressions.

Opening:
1. If possible, have recent visitors to your congregation meet with your group to share some of their impressions about your church and about how they have been welcomed thus far.

OR—Ask group members to brainstorm two lists, and write the responses on a chalkboard or some newsprint. The first list should cover reasons why visitors should feel good about your congregation and want to return. The second list should cover reasons why visitors may not be interested in returning.

Looking into the Scripture:
2. Before reading the Scripture, ask class members to put themselves in the position of Zacchaeus as they listen to the story. Point out that Zacchaeus had been recruited by the Romans to collect taxes from the Jews. When such appointed collectors were able to obtain tax revenue beyond a defined level, they could keep the excess for themselves. Consequently tax collectors were motivated to be harsh in their dealings, and they were despised by almost everyone. Then read or have a volunteer read **Luke 19:1–10.** Discuss:
  • How did Jesus first find you: up a tree, out on a limb, ...?
  • Do you think Jesus' words in verses 9–10 stopped the crowd's muttering? Why, or why not? On what basis did Jesus confirm the salvation of Zacchaeus?
  • How can we, like Jesus, help persons in the position of the outsider?

Looking into *Widening the Welcome of Your Church*:
3. Focus attention on the chart on page 37 about the reasons for which people visit a church the first time. Discuss:
  • Are you surprised by the fact that the invitation or encouragement of friends plays such a major role? Why, or why not?
  • Do any of the other percentages surprise you? Why, or why not?
  • What changes in attitude would the chart suggest are needed in your congregation?

Study Guide – Page 196

- What makes us reluctant to personally invite people to church? How can our motivation be improved?

4. Focus attention on the chart on page 45 about the reasons for visitors returning to a church for more visits after the initial one. Discuss:
- Look at the fuller wording of the items on the chart as those appear at the bottom of page 45 and on page 46. Which of those would people be likely to experience in your congregation? Why? Which of those would people be unlikely to experience in your congregation? Why?
- Note the important words near the middle of page 46: "We are not simply talking about a change in program or strategy. We are talking about a fundamental change in attitude toward those outside the church and toward those who come to the church as visitors." What do those words mean for you personally? What do they mean for your congregation?

5. Read aloud the words about a vision of hospitality that appear in the box on page 48. What would it mean for your church to have a vision of hospitality? List items on a chalkboard or some newsprint.

Closing:
6. Close with a prayer for God's guidance in helping a vision of hospitality and the practice of hospitality become real for your entire congregation.

Challenge: Observe a worship service in your church from the perspective of a visitor. Identify at least one aspect of the service which would be potentially confusing to a visitor. Decide on a solution to that problem, and share it with the appropriate person or committee in the church.

Session Five:
Experiencing Hospitality in the Church

Widening the Welcome of Your Church **Reference:**
Experiencing Hospitality in the Church (pages 51–62). Make cards
in advance for the opening activity, describing various visitors.
Make copies for group members of "How do you and the church
respond to. . ." which follows this session plan.
***Biblical* Focus: Matthew 26:6–13** (Jesus in the home of a
leper).

Opening:
1. Have each of the following descriptions on a notecard,
and give that notecard to a person in the group. Then ask those
persons to describe what it is like to visit your church from the
perspective of the identity given on the card. The identity should
be read aloud before the description is given.

Card One: You are a single parent with one young child.
You have lived in the community for two years
but have never attended this church before.

Card Two: You are retired, and your spouse died last year.
You haven't been involved in a congregation for
many years, but you are feeling a need to deepen
your faith.

Card Three: You are middle-aged. You actually belonged to
this church many years ago but dropped out
because you thought the minister and some
members were too cold. Now you've decided to
give the church a try again.

Card Four: You're a teenager visiting on your own. Your
parents don't belong to any church and think
you're crazy for coming. You've only been in a
worship service two or three times when you were
a young child and have had little contact with
the church. Things that have happened with
friends at school have caused you to want to
grow closer to God, and you think you need help
from the church.

Card Five: You're in your early thirties, married, and have
just moved into the community. You were very
active in a church of another denomination
before the move, but this is the closest church to
your new home.

Card Six: You're in your late thirties, married, and have just
moved into the community. You haven't been
active in a church since you were in junior high
school. Because you have three children, you've

been thinking that you should start attending.

Looking into the Scripture:
2. Have **Matthew 26:6–13** read aloud with persons taking these parts: narrator, Jesus, woman with the ointment, and a disciple questioning what has happened. Discuss:
- The identity of Simon the leper is unknown. Why do you suppose Jesus chose to be in the home of a leper?
- The woman showed great hospitality to Jesus. Why did the disciples react negatively to what she did? What does the response of Jesus say about his own life and death? What does the response of Jesus say concerning the practice of hospitality?

Looking into *Widening the Welcome of Your Church*:
3. Be prepared to summarize the experiences of Madeline, Brad and Ann (plus two daughters and one son), and Eddie as shared in pages 51–53 and 58–61. How would your congregation respond to persons like these? Try listing on a chalkboard or some newsprint the positive responses that would come and the negative responses that might also come. What are the kinds of visitors with which your church does the best job? What kinds of visitors are most likely to feel uncomfortable in your congregation?

4. Focus attention on the definitions of stranger, foreigner, alien, and sojourner that appear on page 56. What are the different needs which those persons would have? How would persons in those categories experience the welcome of our congregation?

5. Have people work in pairs to complete "How do you and the church respond to. . . ." Then invite each pair to share one or two observations with the whole group.

Closing:
6. Pages 61–62 discuss the importance of "Creating Places for People to Belong." Have each person share one change needed in your church to create more places for people to belong, and then close with prayer.

Challenge: Invite two households to have dinner or dessert with you on the same evening: one household which has been part of the church for many years and one which has only recently joined. If having them in your home isn't convenient, then arrange to have dinner or dessert together at a restaurant.

How do you and the church respond to. . .

- The person who is present every week and who has several close friends in the church? (This probably describes most people reading this book!)

- The person who is regular in attendance but whose closest friends are outside of the congregation?

- The person who attends only on an occasional basis and doesn't feel tightly bonded to the congregation?

- The person who has become chronically inactive and rarely attends?

- The visitor who already knows several members?

- The visitor who knows almost no one in the congregation except the person who extended the invitation to come?

- The visitor who has just moved to the area and truly knows no one in the congregation?

Session Six:
Welcoming Strangers

Widening the Welcome of Your Church **Reference:**
Welcoming Strangers (pages 63–72). Paper and pencils for the
first activity. Copies of "What We Want When We Are Strangers"
(pages 67–72) for each person in the group (so people don't have
to write in their books).
Biblical Focus: Hebrews 13:2 (practicing hospitality and
entertaining angels without being aware of it).

Opening:
1. Have group members draw floor plans for their present
homes or of their childhood homes. A sample appears below.
Have people share the plans and talk about their attitudes
toward the home in groups of three to five persons.

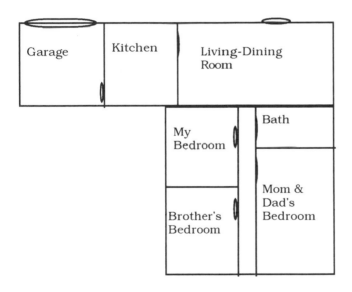

Then summarize the material on attitudes about the home
and attitudes toward strangers on pages 64–65. Invite group
members to share how their attitudes toward the home have
helped shape their attitudes toward strangers.

Looking into the Scripture:
2. Read aloud **Hebrews 13:2**. Discuss:
 • If we truly believed this passage of Scripture, how would
 that change our attitudes toward strangers?

- Read aloud the boldfaced statement at the bottom of page 66. How is that statement consistent with Hebrews 13:2? Why are Hebrews 13:2 and the statement on page 66 of importance to churches wanting to practice hospitality?

Looking into *Widening the Welcome of Your Church*:

3. Number off (1, 2, 3 or 1, 2, 3, 4, 5 or. . .) so that approximately one-fifth of your group will have the same number. Have all ones leave the room. Those still in the room should select a topic for a discussion which will begin a minute before the ones return to the room. The others should intentionally try to keep the ones shut out of the discussion, and should not even announce the topic to them. Possible topics:

- Where people would like to go on vacation if money were no object.
- The motion picture that people think was the best one to be released in recent months.
- The television show that people think is the worst one of the season.
- Reasons why the church ought to purchase a new car as a gift for the pastor.

Begin the discussion, bring the ones back into the room, and continue the discussion. Stop the discussion after three to five more minutes. Ask the ones to share how it felt to come into the room in the middle of a discussion. Ask the others whether it felt easy or difficult to shut the others out. What can we learn from this concerning the way that strangers feel when they start coming to classes and groups in our congregations?

4. Pass out copies of "What We Want When We Are Strangers." Have people work in groups of three to five to go through the items, checking those which need more attention by the church and/or by individuals. Invite each small group to share a few observations with the total group.

Closing:

5. Close with a prayer of thanksgiving for the gift of strangers.

Challenge: Go out of your way to extend welcome to a stranger—at church if possible and also in another setting (your neighborhood, at work, in a community meeting, . . .).

Session Seven:
Welcoming Children

Widening the Welcome of Your Church **Reference:** Welcoming Children (pages 73–90). Copies for the group of "Strategies for Greater Hospitality to Children." You'll want volunteers for the skit in step two, and you'll need copies of the skit or photocopies of this page for them.

Biblical **Focus: Mark 10:13–16** ("Let the little children come to me").

Optional Preparation: Arrange for one or more children (elementary grades 1, 2, 3, or 4) to be present.

Opening:

1. Visit with the children who've been invited to come about their view of the church. How welcome do they feel at worship services? At the coffee or fellowship time? In Sunday school? At other church events? How good a job are they doing of helping new students feel welcome?

OR—Share a summary of Jessica's experiences (pages 73–76), and then invite group members to talk about what it would be like for a child to visit your church. You may wish to put responses on a chalkboard or some newsprint.

Looking into the Scripture:

2. Use a skit to introduce **Mark 10:13–16**. Have volunteers (or draftees if necessary) take the part of characters from biblical times. Let people change the lines if they wish to do so.

Mother:	(Carrying a child) Lord, it would mean a great deal to me if you would bless my child.
Jesus:	(Reaching out and touching the child) May God's gracious love and peace remain with you.
Grandfather:	(Carrying a child) Rabbi, please bless my grandchild.
Disciple:	(Stepping between the grandfather and Jesus) I'm sorry, but you'll have to step back. You're crowding the Lord. Get out of the way.
Grandfather:	I didn't think I was crowding Jesus, and the blessing is so important to myself and the infant's mother.
Disciple:	Don't argue with me. You're just wasting time. We have more important things to do than this.
Jesus:	(Moving between the disciple and the grandfather) Enough. "'Let the little children

Study Guide – Page 203

come to me; do not stop them; for it is to such as these that the kingdom 'of God belongs.'"

Then have people read Mark 10:13–16. Ask:
- What does this passage say about the importance of children?
- What is the difference between having a child-like attitude and being childish?
- What do we lose when we no longer have the ability to view life as children?

Looking into *Widening the Welcome of Your Church*:
3. Focus attention on the chart on page 79 of *Widening the Welcome of Your Church*. The chart shows the attitudes toward children reflected in program offerings and strategies in over three hundred congregations. Go through the items, utilizing the commentary on pages 78–81 as background, and compare your congregation with those which participated in the study.

4. Give copies of "Strategies for Greater Hospitality to Children" to group members. Have them work in groups of three to five persons to identify the five strategies that would be of greatest help to your congregation in improving its outreach and welcome to children; see pages 81–90 for further background on those strategies Give the small groups opportunity to share results with the total group.

Closing:
5. Close with a prayer thanking God for the gift of children and asking God's help in being more childlike in our worship and faithfulness.

Challenge: Spend some time with children this week. If you don't have any children or if they've grown, find a nephew, niece, grandchild, or neighbor. If you visit with children who are not active in a local church, consider inviting them to share in activities at your congregation and offering to provide transportation.

Strategies for Greater Hospitality to Children

Check the five strategies below which would be of greatest importance to your congregation in improving its hospitality to children:

___ 1. The church needs to evaluate the nursery and child care areas from the perspective of children and their parents.

___ 2. Sunday school classes (or other Christian education settings) should also be evaluated from the standpoint of children and parents.

___ 3. Greeters and ushers need training in how to respond to children.

___ 4. The worship service should also respond to the needs of children.

___ 5. The needs of children should be taken into consideration during any kind of fellowship time.

___ 6. Familiar faces are important to children!

___ 7. Being known by one's own name is important!

___ 8. Discipline problems, when they arise, need to be handled with tact and consideration.

___ 9. With children, as with adults, it's important for a quick response to be made when there is a break in regular attendance.

___ 10. When a church has a day care or nursery school program through the week, opportunities should be sought for the church to show hospitality to those children and their parents.

___ 11. Be sensitive to children with special needs.

___ 12. Be alert for additional program opportunities that can help meet the needs of children.

___ 13. Be sure that your promotional materials and strategies make it clear that children are valued in your congregation!

___ 14. Involve children who are already in your church in helping you evaluate your programs.

___ 15. Provide opportunities for children to interact with older members of the congregation.

Session Eight:
Welcoming Teenagers

Widening the Welcome of Your Church **Reference:** *Welcoming Teenagers* (pages 91–102). Copies for the group of "What It Means To Welcome Youth."

Biblical Focus: 1 Corinthians 13:1–13 (Paul's classic poem about love).

Optional Preparation: Have one or more teenagers come to share with your group. OR—Tape a teenage discussion segment from MTV.

Opening:
1. Visit with teenagers from your church about how welcoming they feel your congregation is to persons their age. How do they feel when they attend worship? How do they feel in Sunday school? How do they feel during fellowship time? How do they feel at events for people of all ages?

OR—Show a videotape of a discussion by teenagers on MTV. Then ask group members to identify factors that would be important for a congregation that truly wanted to welcome young people like those on the videotape.

OR—Ask group members to identify what it would be like for a teenager to visit your church. List observations on a chalkboard or some newsprint.

Looking into the Scripture:
2. Point out to group members that the verses just before the famous words in **1 Corinthians 13:1–13** are concerned with spiritual gifts. The greatest gift is not speaking in tongues or prophecy but love. Have a volunteer read the thirteenth chapter of 1 Corinthians aloud, and then discuss:
* Why is love so important in the lives of all people? How does loving help connect us to God?
* Teenagers go through many transitions. What role should love play in those transitions from the point of view of the church?

Looking into *Widening the Welcome of Your Church*:
3. Put two columns on a chalkboard or some newsprint. In the column on the left, list words or phrases group members share to describe their own teenage years. In the column on the right, list words or phrases which describe teenage life today. Refer to pages 93–100 as appropriate for further background on life for today's teens.

4. Give group members copies of "What It Means To Welcome Youth." Have them divide into groups of three to five persons to go through the strategies or ideas which are listed. Have each small group place a check by the items which need further development in your congregation. Then have each small group briefly share observations with the total group.

Closing:
5. Close with a prayer of thanksgiving for the gifts that teenagers bring to the church and for guidance in creating an atmosphere that is truly welcoming for teenagers.

Challenge: Spend some time with teenagers this week. If you don't have any teenagers at home, find a nephew, niece, grandchild, or neighbor in the teen years. If you visit with young people who are not active in a local church, consider inviting them to share in activities at your congregation and offering to provide transportation if needed.

What It Means To Welcome Youth

___ Welcoming congregations appreciate the fact that youth are not just the "church of tomorrow" but are in fact part of the church today.

___ Welcoming congregations recognize that it is crucial to provide an accepting atmosphere for teens, regardless of superficial matters such as hairstyle and clothing.

___ Welcoming congregations take very seriously the need to provide a "safe place" for youth.

___ Welcoming congregations offer a balance of opportunities for youth but also recognize that some teens will be more comfortable with one or two kinds of activities than with others.

___ Opportunity to share in worship and to give leadership to congregational services.

___ Opportunity to learn.

___ Opportunity for recreation and social activities.

___ Opportunity for service.

___ Welcoming congregations teach youth about hospitality and how to welcome others.

___ Welcoming congregations appreciate the role food can play for youth just as it does for adults.

___ Welcoming congregations have had considerable success with mentoring programs in which adults are paired with youth.

___ Welcoming congregations have learned the crucial role that small group sharing should play in youth work.

Session Nine:
Welcoming Young Adults

Widening the Welcome of Your Church **Reference:** *Welcoming Young Adults* (pages 103–118). Copies for group members of "Welcoming Young Adults."
Biblical Focus: **1 John 4:13–21** (classic words about love).
Optional Preparation: Have one or more young adults (18–35 years of age) present to share with your group.

Opening:
1. Visit with young adults from your church about how welcoming they feel your congregation is to persons their age. How do they feel when they attend worship? How do they feel in Sunday school? How do they feel during fellowship time? How do they feel at events for people of all ages?

OR—Ask group members to identify and list on some newsprint or a chalkboard:
• The various life situations of young adults. For example:
— Single, in college   — Single, in trade school
— Married, in college   — Married, in trade school
— Single, working   — Married, working
— Single, no children — Divorced with two children
— ....   — ....

• What it would be like for young adults to visit your congregation? Which categories of young adults are most likely to feel good about what happens in your congregation?

Looking into the Scripture:
2. Read, or have a volunteer read aloud **1 John 4:13–21.** Discuss:
• The biblical selection for the previous session plan on teenagers was 1 Corinthians 13:1–13. Why do you think passages emphasizing love were chosen for each of these topics (teenagers and young adults)?
• What help do these words offer to churches which are experiencing significant conflict between young adults and older adults?

Looking into *Widening the Welcome of Your Church*:
3. Go through the perspectives on young adults provided on pages 106–114. As you do so, identify which ones are true for your congregation.

4. Share copies of "Welcoming Young Adults" with group members. Have people work in groups of three to five persons to
Study Guide – Page 209

go through the list of recommendations and check those that should be implemented in your congregation. Provide a few minutes for the small groups to share reports with the total group.

5. Summarize or read relevant portions of "Young Adults and Church Structure" from pages 117–118. How is your church doing on the characteristics of structure that have often been identified in growing congregations (page 118)? How many of these are true for your church?

- A structure that emphasizes DOING more than DECIDING.
- A structure with fewer standing committees and more task forces or mission groups appointed as needs arise.
- A greater willingness to trust individuals and groups to make decisions without having several decision-making layers.
- A clearer separation of those decisions which have significant impact on the whole congregation and those which are of relatively minor importance.

Decide on the group to which your results should be reported and do so.

Closing:
6. Close with prayer thanking God for the gift of persons of all ages and seeking guidance for your congregation in becoming a more welcoming place.

Challenge: Share a meal with a young adult single, couple, or family. If you're a young adult, then invite another young adult household to join you. If possible, reach out to someone who is inactive in the congregation or who is unchurched.

Welcoming Young Adults

___ Helping older adults in the church better understand the perspective of young adults both inside and outside of the church.

___ Implement as many of the suggestions as possible from the chapter on *Welcoming Children.*

___ Help members of the congregation be sure that they are just as welcoming to young singles and to couples who do not have children as they are to young couples with children.

___ Make a special effort to help older members understand the unique circumstances of single parents.

___ Recognize the need for variety in worship services.

___ Be prepared to more quickly integrate enthusiastic young adults into the life of the church.

___ If your church is to be sensitive to the needs of young adults on a continuing basis, then you need to have persons of that age range as members of the major decision-making groups in your congregation.

___ Recognize the reality that young adults who have not grown up in the church may not be familiar with many things that the rest of us take for granted.

___ Provide many opportunities for young adults and older adults to interact with one another.

Session Ten:
Hospitality and the Overlooked

Widening the Welcome of Your Church **Reference:** *Hospitality and the Overlooked* (pages 119–136). Volunteers for the drama or skit in step one.
Biblical Focus: Luke 14:7–14 (inviting the poor, the crippled, the lame, and the blind to a banquet).

Opening:
1. Begin with a skit about the tendencies of our congregations to reach out only to persons very much like those who are already members. The initial lines are given, but the participants may wish to continue or improvise using their own creativity.

Member #1: The pastor said this morning that we're supposed to reach more people who are different than we are.

Member #2: What did he mean by different?

Member #1: You know, like more of us work as teachers than any other occupational category. We're also almost all white. We simply tend to invite people to church who are just like us.

Member #2: But suppose you invited someone who was younger than most of our adult members, black, and a resident in another part of town. Who would talk to that person? Wouldn't that person feel so out of place that he or she would want to leave?

Member #1: Yes, that's probably true, but that's why we need to make changes to become more accepting and open.

Member #2: But then people will come who aren't just like us.

Member #1: And what would be wrong with that? . . . .

Member #2: . . . .

Looking into the Scripture:
2. Read or have a volunteer read **Luke 14:7–14**. Then discuss:
- Based on this passage, would Jesus support our tendency to only reach persons very much like ourselves?
- Why is it beneficial to do things for persons who cannot repay us? What is wrong with seeking new members primarily to increase the financial base of the church?
- What are the rewards of reaching out to persons who are different from us?

Study Guide – Page 212

Looking into *Widening the Welcome of Your Church*:
3. Focus attention on the descriptions of Karen and of Nate and Taina (on pages 120–121). Why did these persons have such high anxiety about how accepted they would be in a congregation? Invite group members to talk about their friendships or family connections with unmarried persons who are living together and with persons of nonheterosexual orientation. How do you feel about outreach to unmarried persons who are living together and to persons of nonheterosexual orientation? How could your congregation become more welcoming to such persons?

4. Focus attention on pages 124–126 on differences between persons in the neighborhood immediately around the church and the overall membership of the church. The chart on page 125 may be helpful in understanding this material. In what ways does your church face some of the limitations shared in these pages? How could you more effectively reach out to the neighborhood around the church?

5. Divide into small groups. Have each group look through the list on pages 126–132 and then develop their own list of persons likely to be overlooked by your church.

Have each small group report to the total group, and put the results on chalkboard or newsprint. Then decide on a couple of categories for more emphasis in the outreach of your congregation. Discuss:

*   How can you more effectively extend the church's welcome to those persons before they start attending? How can you help them feel genuinely welcome when they begin attending?
*   Are there categories of people your church may not be able to successfully reach? If so, what are they and why?
*   Categories are useful in organizing our thoughts and developing strategies. What are the shortcomings of thinking about people in terms of categories? What differences may exist between your response to a given individual and your response to a category of persons?

Closing:
6. Close with a prayer of thanksgiving for the gift of all those persons who are seeking to grow closer to God.

Challenge: Find a person who has been overlooked in terms of outreach by your congregation and get better acquainted with that individual. Seek to involve that person in the life of your church.

Session Eleven:
How Welcoming Are Your Physical Facilities?

Widening the Welcome of Your Church Reference: *How Welcoming Are Your Physical Facilities?* (pages 137–148). Copies for group members of "A Checklist on Physical Facilities." Make whatever arrangements are needed so that your class can take a tour of your church's physical facilities. If your group meets on a weekday evening, you may not need to make any arrangements! If you meet on Sunday morning, you may want to let other classes know about the tour so that they will not be perplexed as you go by or upset if you briefly look into the door of a classroom. If a group meets in the sanctuary at the same time as your group, then you may want to ask their permission to walk into the sanctuary for a few minutes. **Biblical Focus: Luke 2:41–51** (on Jesus in the temple).

Opening:
1. Start the session by taking a tour of the physical facilities of your church. Weather permitting, start the tour from the church's parking lot (or if your church doesn't have a parking lot, from the place where most automobiles are parked). Encourage group members to view the physical facilities as though they were first-time visitors to the congregation. Encourage people to make notes that can be used for discussion. You'll also find plenty of discussion happening during the tour!

If you are in a very small building, then this activity may take just a few minutes. If you are in a very large building or on a multi-building campus, then you may not have time to see everything. Try not to let this opening activity take more than fifty percent of your meeting time. Be sure to include the sanctuary, one or more children's classrooms, a youth meeting room or area, at least one other adult classroom, the main church kitchen, a lounge or parlor area if you have one, the church office, and at least one restroom.

Looking into the Scripture:
2. Read or have a volunteer read **Luke 2:41–51.** Discuss:
* What, if anything, can we tell from this passage about the physical facilities in which Jesus as a young boy was teaching? Point out that the Old Testament in fact contains many passages giving building specifications to the Hebrew people but that we do not have comparable sections in the New Testament.
* Jesus referred to the temple as "my Father's house" (v.49). If we think of the church as God's house, what implications does that have for our facilities?

Study Guide – Page 214

- Draw two lines on chalkboard or newsprint and label them like the ones below. Invite group members to quickly come to the front and place their initials at a place on each line which expresses their feelings.

Church buildings should be functional.	Church buildings should be beautiful as well as functional.

As little money as possible should go into church facilities.	The church facilities should be as nice as the church can afford.

Have people talk about their responses. Obviously this exercise oversimplifies the issues, but it should still be useful in stimulating discussion. Talk about the kinds of choices concerning facilities that your church has had to make.

Looking into *Widening the Welcome of Your Church*:
   3. Summarize the material on pages 139–141 on the danger of "Underestimating the Message of the Facilities." Discuss:
   • How does it change our view of the facilities if we think of them as a part of the church's welcome? Does thinking about them from that perspective affect where you placed your initials on either of the lines in the exercise above?
   • Based on your tour, what are some of the major needs of your church as far as physical facilities are concerned?

   4. Have members work in groups of three to five persons to complete the "Checklist on Physical Facilities." Then have the small groups report to the total group, and discuss responses.

Closing:
   5. Identify as a total group the areas from your discussion which most need action, and decide how to share that information with the appropriate persons. You may even decide that there is an improvement that you as a group would like to make to the church to make it a more welcoming place.
   Close with a prayer of thanksgiving for the facilities that are available for the ministry of your church.

Challenge: Ask a visitor or a relatively new member of the church to share with you his or her views on the physical facilities. How beautiful are they? How practical? How welcoming?

A Checklist on Physical Facilities

Check as many of the following statements as apply to the physical facilities of your congregation:

___ Our sanctuary seats far more people than our average worship attendance.

___ Our sanctuary is 80% or more full at most worship services.

___ Our sanctuary doesn't provide an especially attractive setting for worship.

___ Our sanctuary and other facilities aren't "child friendly."

___ Altar furnishings in our sanctuary cannot be arranged to accommodate drama or other innovations in worship.

___ The speaker system in our sanctuary doesn't work well, and a hearing-impaired person would have problems knowing what is happening.

___ We couldn't add classes or groups without expanding our Christian education facilities.

___ Our Christian education classrooms can't really be described as comfortable and attractive.

___ We do not have a comfortable and attractive area for youth.

___ We do not have all the ramps, elevators, and/or other accommodations needed for persons with physical disabilities and other mobility or energy limitations.

___ We need more parking for our congregation.

___ We have plenty of parking, but it isn't paved. We simply park in a dirt or grass lot adjacent to the church.

___ The narthex area or entrance to the sanctuary is fairly small and doesn't encourage visiting by those who come.

___ Our church office facilities feel crowded and/or aren't especially attractive.

___ It's actually a little difficult to find our church.

Session Twelve:
The Changing Shape of Worship and Program

Widening the Welcome of Your Church **Reference:** *The Changing Shape of Worship and Program* (pages 149–160). Copies for the group of the "Congregational Worship Survey."
Biblical Focus: Psalm 100 ("Make a joyful noise to the Lord, all the earth").

Opening:
1. Have people complete the "Congregational Worship Survey." Then invite them to go back through the survey as though they had been first-time visitors to the last worship service they attended. Have them mark those items where being a visitor could make a difference in response. Talk as a total group about the results.

Looking into the Scripture:
2. Read aloud **Psalm 100.** Discuss:
- Using this Psalm as the basis, what would you say is the purpose of worship?
- We have a tendency to evaluate worship in terms of our personal preferences and in terms of how well it speaks to us as individuals. Is such a view consistent with the perspective of Psalm 100? Why, or why not?

Looking into *Widening the Welcome of Your Church*:
3. Summarize for the group the perspective given on pages 149–154 on "Creating Comfort in Worship." The boldfaced paragraph at the bottom of page 152 and the two points at the top of page 153 merit particular emphasis. Discuss:
- Why does preoccupation with our own needs make it difficult to focus on the needs of visitors?
- What are the rewards of focusing more on the needs of visitors than on our own needs? Does it require greater maturity in the faith or greater security as a person to focus on the needs of others more than on our own needs? Why, or why not?
- The top of page 153 raises two different directions in worship as possibilities for congregations focusing on hospitality. Which of those directions seems most realistic for your congregation? Is there a third direction that would be better for your church?

4. Assign each of the following sections from *The Changing Shape of Worship and Program* to a small group. Ask each group to look at its assigned section, talk about the issues raised, and

Study Guide – Page 217

prepare a summary of the implications of that section for your congregation.

- "A Caution" (pages 154–155)
- "Baptism and Church Membership" (pages 156)
- "Prayer and Prayer Rooms" (pages 157)
- "Listening as Vital to Hospitality and Program" (pages 159–160)

Have the small groups share their summaries with the total group.

Closing:

5. Focus attention on the "What Next?" section (pages 133–134). Look at the definition of hospitality and the Hebrews verse at the end of the chapter.

If this is your final session, have group members reflect briefly on what they have learned through this study.

If you will be doing Session 13 next week, have group members identify additional areas they would like to discuss and read the chapter *Hospitality Checkups and Congregational Studies.*

Close with prayer.

Challenge: Extend a welcome to an unchurched person in your neighborhood, at your place of work, or in another community context, and invite that person to worship with you next week. If each person in your study group does this, there should be many opportunities for you to practice welcoming skills next week!

Congregational Worship Survey

- Are you a (check one)
  ___first-time visitor? ___repeat visitor? ___member?
- How would you rate the overall quality of the worship service (check one)?
  ___ Poor ___ Fair ___ Good ___ Excellent
- Is the service (check one)
  ___ too long? ___ too short? ___ just right?
- How would you rate the appearance of the sanctuary (check one)?
  ___ Poor ___ Fair ___ Good ___ Excellent
  Please write any suggestions for improvement on the reverse side.
- Are instructions for child care, communion, the offering collection, and other elements of the service clear?
  ___Yes ___No Please list anything which was unclear:
  _____
- Were your physical needs met in regard to:
  temperature? ___Yes ___No
  lighting? ___Yes ___No
  bulletin? ___Yes ___No
  sound? ___Yes ___No
  seating? ___Yes ___No
- Did you feel welcome? ___Yes ___No If not, was there anything in particular that made you feel unwelcome?
  _____
- How would you rate the music?
  ___ Poor ___ Fair ___ Good ___ Excellent
  Write on the reverse side any songs or hymns you would like used.
- Did the service flow smoothly? ___Yes ___No
  Did it seem unified? ___Yes ___No If not, what didn't fit? _____
- Check the worship variations you would find meaningful:
  ___ drama ___ contemporary Christian music
  ___ use of video ___ contemporary prayers
- How do you feel about the amount of congregational participation?
  ___ The right amount ___ Not enough ___ Too much
- How would you rate the sermon in regard to:
  content? ___ Poor ___ Fair ___ Good ___ Excellent
  delivery? ___ Poor ___ Fair ___ Good ___ Excellent
  length? ___ Too long ___ Just right ___ Too short
  Write on the reverse side any themes, problems in life, or biblical passages you like to see addressed in the sermon.

Session Thirteen:
What Next?

*This session is designed as a wrap-up to your study of **Widening the Welcome of Your Church** and will probably not be utilized by some groups. It provides an opportunity to set goals for next steps in widening the welcome of your church. It relates somewhat to the chapter on "Hospitality Checkups and Congregational Studies."*

1. Share snacks with the group, much as was done for the first session in the study. Talk informally about what people have gained from this study.

2. Focus the attention of group members on the chapter *Hospitality Checkups and Congregational Studies.* Which of the strategies shared there seem of the greatest potential help to your congregation? What group or groups in the church should be asked to pursue those strategies?

3. Have group members look again at the biblical quote found on page 8 of **Widening the Welcome of Your Church** and at the definition of hospitality on page 22. In light of those quotes and the study as a whole, talk together about:

- The next steps that need to be taken by people individually in becoming more welcoming. Invite as many as are willing to share their plans.

- The next steps your class or group should take. If this has been a short-term group for the purpose of studying this book, then there may not be next steps for the group. If that is the case, think about ways group members can have impact on other groups and organizations in the church.

- The next steps which your congregation as a whole should take. Develop some specific strategies for influencing others.

4. Close with a prayer of thanksgiving for the welcome Christ has extended to all of us!

About Christian Community And LifeQuest

Christian Community and the publishing imprint of LifeQuest are committed to finding practical strategies that help churches with the pressing issues of our time. We do careful research and field-testing so that we know the strategies we offer will work in churches like yours. We have no interest in manipulation, gimmicks, or overly simplistic answers to complex problems.

Our research and development projects have been concerned with topics such as:

- Improving the hospitality of congregations
- Developing strategies for improved congregational outreach
- Relating stewardship directly to the spiritual life
- Expanding opportunities for planned giving to local congregations
- Conducting congregational surveys and helping churches and judicatories relate the survey information to strategic planning
- Helping churches move beyond tensions between contemporary and traditional approaches to worship
- Understanding how the religious faith of teens relates to their sexual values and behavior
- Understanding the different ways that young adults and older adults view the church and society

We are also committed to cooperative work with others. We have involved churches of over thirty different denominations in our research and development projects, and we often work cooperatively with regional and national denominational officials. We have continuing partnerships with New Life Ministries; the Religious Institute for Sexual Morality, Justice, and Healing; and the Network for Charitable Giving.

To order resources or for more information about our organization, you can contact us at:

> **Christian Community**
> **6404 S. Calhoun Street**
> **Fort Wayne, Indiana 46807**
> **For orders: 800–774–3360**
> **E-mail: DadofTia@aol.com**
> **www.churchstuff.com**

More on Hospitality from Christian Community

The First Thirty Seconds: A Guide to Hospitality for Greeters and Ushers by S. Joan Hershey. Greeters and ushers are the "first contact" with the congregation for many who visit. The number one question visitors want answered is: "Is this a friendly congregation?" This booklet offers clear training for greeters and ushers, with an emphasis on hospitality. Giving copies to all greeters and ushers in your church can help widen your church's welcome.

Hospitality: Life in a Time of Fear by Steve Clapp & Fred Bernhard. This book deals directly with the tough questions raised by the tragic events of September 11, 2001, and reveals that the answer to fear is not turning inward but turning outward. Learning to recognize the presence of Christ in others can have a liberating impact on all that we do and can enable us to move past the fears that threaten to immobilize us. This is an excellent guide to the development of hospitality as a part of the spiritual life and shows how hospitality relates to our faith, our homes, our neighborhoods, our places of work, and even our driving. Includes discussion questions for classes and small groups.

Invite a Friend Kit by S. Joan Hershey. This kit will provide you with a thorough step-by-step action plan for an "Invite a Friend Sunday." The kit includes five copies of the booklet *A Guide to an Effective Invite a Friend Sunday* as well as a timeline for planning the event, ideas for engaging con-gregational participation, and sample printed resources.

Public Relations Kit: Help from a Hospitality Perspective by Kristen Leverton Helbert and Dick Benner. Media exposure and publicity can play a valuable role not only in a church's evangelistic efforts but also in its outreach ministries. This practical kit, which comes with permission to photocopy, shares how the Internet, newspapers, radio, television, direct mail, the yellow pages, the telephone, the appearance of the church, and the attitudes of people can all contribute to the church as a place of hospitality.

Worship and Hospitality by Steve Clapp & Fred Bernhard. Looks at worship through the lens of hospitality. This book is an effort to move beyond the tension among traditional, contemporary, and blended worship to create worship which speaks to the deepest needs of people and builds up the church as the body of Christ. A guide for individual or group study is included.